India's Bravehearts

A Note on the Author

Lieutenant General Satish Dua (Retired), PVSM, UYSM, SM, VSM, retired as the Chief of Integrated Defence Staff. As the Corps Commander in Srinagar, he planned and executed the surgical strikes in Kashmir in 2016. A counter-terrorism specialist from 8 JAK LI (Siachen), he has operated extensively in J&K and the Northeast during his four decades of service. He has also been a Commando Instructor and India's Defence Attaché in Vietnam, Cambodia and Laos.

India's Bravehearts

Untold Stories from the Indian Army

Lieutenant General Satish Dua (Retired)

JUGGERNAUT BOOKS
C-I-128, First Floor, Sangam Vihar, Near Holi Chowk,
New Delhi 110080, India

First published by Juggernaut Books 2020

Copyright © Lieutenant General Satish Dua (Retired) 2020

10 9 8 7 6 5 4 3 2

P-ISBN: 9789353451370
E-ISBN: 9789353451387

The views and suggestions expressed in this book are by
the author in his personal capacity only.

All rights reserved. No part of this publication may be reproduced,
transmitted, or stored in a retrieval system in any form or by any
means without the written permission of the publisher.

Typeset in Adobe Caslon Pro by R. Ajith Kumar, Noida

Printed at Thomson Press India Ltd

To the brave Indian Soldier, who asks for so little, yet is always willing and ready to risk his life for the country

Contents

Foreword ix
Preface xi

1. Surgical Strike Across the LoC 1
2. Leading from the Front 31
3. Life on the LoC 55
4. Main aur Meri Helmet 71
5. That Was Close! 85
6. A Woman in the Village 105
7. If You Get There Alive, You Will Live 117
8. Don't Call the Soldier 127
9. Catching a Snake 141
10. Tough Times Don't Last, Tough People Do 155
11. The Making of a Hero 169
12. Bad News 185

Afterword 195
Acknowledgements 199

Foreword

Lieutenant General Satish Dua is a comrade-at-arms and a dear friend with whom I have spent quite some time, on and off the beaten track. A leader of men, he has had an outstanding career commanding troops from the icy heights of Kashmir to the thick jungles of the Northeast where he has matched steel and wits with our adversaries, external and internal. It gives me immense pleasure to present his book *India's Bravehearts*, filled to the brim with memories and anecdotes, and an ode to the quintessential Indian soldier – a life lived extraordinarily.

The tales of bravery and bravado of Indian soldiers recounted in this book warm the hearts and steel the nerves. I hope they will ignite the minds of

Foreword

all readers, especially our younger generation who look towards the Olive Greens for inspiration and guidance. For those already donning the colour and out of it, this is a trip down memory lane.

A better narrator than Lieutenant General Satish Dua could not have been found, and in this book he displays his writing prowess too. I wish him all the best for the success of his book.

Jai Hind.

(M.M. Naravane)
General

Preface

I was ten or eleven years old when I decided I wanted to join the army. At the age of sixteen I had already secured a seat in a medical college, when I got the call letter giving me admission to the National Defence Academy (NDA). So I did the first semester of MBBS, then came home and convinced my parents to let me switch. I have never regretted it.

I did reasonably well at the Academy, became a Commando Instructor and eventually retired as a Lieutenant General in the army, specializing in counter-terrorism. You may not know my name, but you would know of one of the last operations I

Preface

oversaw as Corps Commander – the surgical strike of 2016 in Kashmir, in response to the terror attack at Uri.

I gave the armed forces thirty-nine years of my life. I had my successes as well as my share of upsets in military operations. I had close shaves and survived, while sadly some of my dear comrades did not. And I made a village of close friends. This is the soldier's life. This is my story.

My story is also the story of an army officer who learnt how to live and train and go into battle with soldiers. Who learnt how to plan operations so that innocent bystanders didn't get hurt, lead troops boldly, take decisions even when there were no clear directions, deal with emotions and hide his own fears. As I always say, counter-terrorism is the trickiest operation – it is like playing chess with live bullets.

Every infantry officer aspires to command the unit he has been commissioned in and hopes to

Preface

get an opportunity to lead his soldiers in combat. I was fortunate to get to do both in the summer of 1998. That year I was promoted to the rank of a Colonel and was appointed as the Commanding Officer (CO) of my own battalion of the Jammu and Kashmir Light Infantry, 8 JAK LI (Siachen), which has the official honour of 'Bravest of the Brave'. Our unit was deployed in an operationally active area on the Line of Control (LoC) in Jammu and Kashmir (J&K).

This is a collection of stories mostly from my days as a CO – they are stories of operations, risks taken, lucky escapes, extraordinary colleagues; and of the unseen aspects of the soldier's life, from the rigorous training to the outstanding hospitals that ensure we can return to battle and serve our country again.

Those years in command taught me life lessons, tactics and empathy; they made me emotionally sensitive, and at times ruthless; they taught me to put faith in my soldiers and in God and recognize

Preface

the power of positive thinking. Above all, they taught me that when things seem uncertain and the path is unclear, one has to take a leap of faith and aim high. My officers, my soldiers and my gut instinct never let me down.

I hope you enjoy these stories.

Jai Hind!

1
Surgical Strike Across the LoC

Dawn was yet to break when the shrill ringing of the phone woke me up. It was the General Officer Commanding (GOC) of Baramulla Division. 'Our base at Uri has been attacked by terrorists, and I'm afraid, sir, that the situation is rather precarious.'

I was instantly awake. I didn't need to be told how serious this was. If terrorists attacked a military base in person, then they were likely on a suicide mission. And when a man comes prepared to die, he will cause great damage and heavy casualties before he does. The next phone call, a few minutes later, confirmed this.

Thirty minutes later we had all the information. Four suicide terrorists had blazed their way through our base at Uri, very close to the LoC, and caused heavy casualties. During the firefight, a cookhouse also caught fire, which increased the death toll.

In the four decades of my career, I have faced a lot of tough situations, mostly in counter-terrorism. But the scale of what happened on that Sunday, 18 September 2016, was huge. We lost eighteen soldiers.

Eighteen young lives lost. And it happened on my watch. As I got ready to go to the helipad, the cup of tea that I had started sipping suddenly seemed tasteless. I left it and went out to the lawn just to be with myself before the chopper arrived. It was a bright, clear day, but for me it was a dark Sunday, the darkest ever.

The terrorists had chosen their target and timing well. A change of battalion had been in progress. A battalion can stay in a high-altitude area for only two winters. Heights above 9000 feet are considered high altitude, and most of our posts on the LoC ranged from 9000 to 12,000 feet. Soldiers face several medical issues if they stay for prolonged periods at that height, mostly due to lack of oxygen in the air and extreme cold during the snow season.

So the battalion was in the process of moving out, with another one replacing it. During this period of transfer, soldiers of both battalions spend a couple of weeks together to familiarize the incoming troops with the terrain and peculiarities of the LoC. They conduct joint patrolling and lay ambushes together. At this time there are double the usual number of soldiers on all posts. At the Uri base too, there was a concentration of troops from both battalions, with some of them accommodated in tents.

The Uri base therefore proved to be a good target for the suicide terrorists. As they cut the perimeter fence and entered the camp, it was still dark. But they were detected soon and fired upon. Even as one terrorist died, the others dispersed and started firing indiscriminately at sleeping soldiers and those stirring to wakefulness.

It was just before dawn. One of the biggest worries in such situations is coordination. We had soldiers from two different battalions who had not known each other for long. It was also unfortunate that an LPG cylinder exploded inside the cookhouse. The cookhouse went up in flames, which also engulfed a couple of tents.

The scene at Uri was grim. The firing had stopped but the fires were still raging. The casualties, both dead and wounded, had been moved to the field hospital. Sanitization operations to check for more terrorists in the nearby forest were under way. An occasional bullet or grenade would explode because of the heat from the fire.

Meanwhile, news came in that the defence minister, the late Mr Manohar Parrikar, was arriving in Uri that afternoon. 'Why now, why today?' I asked Mr G. Mohan Kumar, the defence secretary, when he rang me up to tell me of the minister's visit.

So many things were happening that needed my attention: the operations in Uri, planning how to fly out the mortal remains of all those who had laid down their lives, the road journey to their home towns, the homage ceremony in Srinagar before their bodies were sent back. So many calls had to be attended to – from the Army Headquarters, the police, the civil administration, the chief minister, the governor. The Army Chief had already arrived. I did not need more VIPs on my hands on a day like this.

When the defence minister arrived, I was struck by the simplicity of the man. But I had to say no to his wish to go to Uri. The operation was still in progress and it was not safe for the minister to be there. He respected the decision. So from the airport we flew by helicopter to Badami Bagh Cantonment in Srinagar, where my headquarters was located.

It was impossible to talk in the noisy chopper. The short flight of ten minutes was the only time I had that day to be alone with my thoughts. It was easy to preach phrases like 'don't despair when there are upsets', 'look for opportunities in every failure', but the attack at Uri was beyond such sentiments.

What could be the hidden opportunity in an operation like this? They always send terrorists across the LoC and we are always defensive and reactive. Then it struck me that there is outrage in the nation, the country is incensed at Pakistan-sponsored terrorism, my soldiers want revenge and there is a bold leadership at the Centre. So why not plan for a strong riposte? Something that had never been done before? Something that can cause the other side hurt and pain in equal measure?

At my headquarters, I finished briefing the defence minister on a map in my operational room. The Army Chief, General Dalbir Singh Suhag, and the Northern Army Commander, Lieutenant

General D.S. Hooda, were also present. Kashmir was my area of responsibility. That is the reason I was doing the talking and briefings. The minister did not interrupt me even once. As I finished giving an account of what had happened so far, he asked, 'So what is the plan now?' I said, 'Sir, if you are asking me about what we can do, then I would like to brief you alone.' 'Yes yes, I would like to talk to you in your chamber,' he said. The officials accompanying the minister did not join as the minister, the Army Chief and the Northern Army Commander walked to my office.

The Army Chief and the Northern Army Commander spoke first. It was their role to work out the larger plans and possibilities at a national level. They talked about our preparedness to take any action and discussed the possibility of our response spiralling into something bigger – that would be beyond my level, as I was in charge of the operational domain only in Kashmir. Mr Parrikar then turned towards me. 'What do you have to say?' I simply said, '*Aap haan keh do, main kar doonga, sir* (You give me the go ahead, and I will do it, sir).' I thought I saw a glint in his eyes, and I knew I had his full attention.

I told him that the Chief would take care of the big picture at the national level; once he gave the green signal, we would plan and execute a bold response on the ground. 'For years, we have been taking a hit when they send in terrorists, and we are unable to react in kind. We will do something which will create that hurt for them too. We will go across the LoC and hit the terrorists' camps inside their territory. But please leave the choice of targets and timings to us.'

For reasons of security, I cannot divulge the details of the operational discussion. What I can reveal is that the defence minister then asked me two quick questions. First, 'There will be no collateral damage, I hope?' I assured him that we should be able to manage that by going through uninhabited areas. In any case, to maintain an element of surprise we would need to keep clear of inhabited areas.

The second was more of a wishful comment. 'There should be no casualties to our own soldiers.' I promptly replied, 'I agree, sir, we should have no casualties, but I cannot guarantee anything. This is war.' He paused for a moment, and my heart sank, thinking how hard a politician would find it to agree to such a thing. He said only one word, *'Barobar!'* This Marathi word has different meanings in different contexts. Here, to me it sounded like 'Great! Let's do it.' When I heard this, for the first time on that dark Sunday I felt a glimmer of satisfaction and relief.

The plan was simple and audacious. We would, in an unprecedented move, raid a few terrorist camps across the LoC, cause heavy casualties and hopefully return with all our men unharmed. Then we would announce to the world and to Pakistan what we had done and why we had done it, unlike Pakistan which always denies that it sends in terrorists. After the minister left, it was agreed that I would discuss the options and possibilities with the Army Commander.

A couple of days later I went to the Command Headquarters to brief the Army Commander, Lieutenant General D.S. Hooda. It was very nice to meet an old friend, Lieutenant General R.R. Nimbhorkar, who was commanding 16 Corps to the south. We go back a long way.

It requires a great deal of planning and coordination for any operation to be successful, especially one as hush-hush and complex as this. The guidance of the Army Commander and his staff, as much as the operational coordination with my friend Nimbhorkar, would be crucial to the success of the operation. I am sure the Army Commander must have kept the Army Chief informed. That is the strength of the army – our hierarchy and chain of command.

The CO of the Special Forces (SF) Battalion was instructed to pick his best teams. That's the way it works in the army. You delegate. The CO knows his commandos best and would pick the right men for the team. For the next ten days we worked like men possessed – planning for various options, weighing the pros and cons of each move, calculating the chances of success against the casualties likely to be incurred, narrowing it down to the options finally adopted, sitting down with the leaders of the teams who would execute the plan and going through every small detail. We also began field training on mock-ups of the target area.

We had chosen terrorist camps that did not have any habitation close by. I recall a prolonged discussion regarding the route in one place where two options existed. I was insisting on the slightly longer route because the shorter option took us a little close to a village. 'The dogs will bark and it can break the surprise,' I said. A few others felt that the village was too far from our route and I was being overcautious at the expense of prolonging our time in the enemy area, which would increase our risk.

I recounted to them my experience in an operation two decades earlier, where the mission was botched because the dogs barking at us from a couple of kilometres distance gave the game away. In a town, the dogs may not bark in the next street, but in the countryside, they will bark from even the next village. As it turned out, the team leader who had to execute this operation agreed with me on this.

On 18 September 2016, when our base at Uri was attacked, the United Nations (UN) General Assembly was in session, and the terrorist attack drew widespread condemnation globally. Pakistan was isolated. Prime Minister Nawaz Sharif's speech in the UN General Assembly was scheduled for 21 September. From that point of view, Pakistan's timing of the terrorist attack at Uri was flawed. There was international pressure on Pakistan to stop supporting terrorism, with an active push from our diplomats.

Our foreign minister, the late Sushma Swaraj, was scheduled to speak on 25 September. We decided to let that day pass peacefully. We also ensured that we did not launch any operations on the next two days, in order to lull the other side into complacency. Meanwhile, during these ten days, we continued to show routine movements and operations all along the front.

We carried out our reconnaissance in the hours of darkness. Several deception measures were used over the next few days, but it would not be prudent to divulge these as then we will not be able to use such measures again. Suffice it to say that our efforts paid off, as the enemy did not have the slightest knowledge of our plans, targets or timings, despite being alert about a possible retaliation from us. If they had any suspicions, these were speculative and they couldn't point a finger to anything specific.

Secrecy is the key to any successful operation. If you catch the enemy unawares, more than half your battle has been won. This is especially the case in a surgical strike where you hit the target, achieve your aim and then have to get out alive. In fact, this is why surgical strikes are the toughest operations in the world. Terrorists infiltrate borders to enter our country. They don't have an exit plan. We had to go in, conduct an operation and get out, all at lightning speed. We had our job cut out for us.

Very few people knew the exact date for the launch of this operation. Everything was strictly on a need-to-know basis. I had expressly forbidden any PowerPoint presentations. If a diagram had to be drawn to explain something, it was to be made in free hand on the spot and destroyed after use. No paper was to be retained by anyone.

We did not even give a name to the operation, because sometimes giving a code name has the opposite effect as people start using the code name and feel secure in their plans. On the day we launched our operation, a few reconnaissance parties had been sent out in advance. They thought that they were going to return at night, but when the operations were launched they were merged with the raid party and moved ahead with them.

Once the mission began, radio communication was kept to the minimum because it is susceptible to interception. I had issued strict instructions that radio sets only be used in an emergency, at least not till the first shot had been fired. Within the teams, however, they could use smaller walkie-talkie sets which have a limited range.

In any case, the commandos, who were highly skilled and seasoned, did not need to keep coordinating with each other. They had perfected this over years of training and working together in different operations. However, they did communicate in code words after crossing pre-decided landmarks known as bounds.

When our control room received a code word, it meant that the commandos had crossed that landmark. We did not ask them for any more details. It was purely one-way communication so that we could follow their real-time progress. Several unarmed vehicles (UAVs) were also used to monitor the progress of our troops. A UAV is a drone minus the weapons – it's a remotely piloted aircraft that can click pictures and videos of a target area and stream them in real time.

We spent an anxious night. I found myself praying more for the safety of our soldiers than for the success of the mission. But somehow I had a positive feeling throughout about this operation. Over the last few days, whenever any of my subordinate staff had voiced their concerns, I had tried to ease their doubts. I told everybody, 'Don't surround yourself with negativity; harness the power of positivity.'

The commandos' progress was slow, painfully

slow, because this was not an operation in the hinterland of Kashmir. They were walking inside enemy territory and faced a hostile atmosphere all around. In operations in the hinterland, hostiles are limited to just a cluster of houses or their hideouts. That was not the case here.

Terrorists' launch pads are usually one or more houses in a village right on the LoC from where they observe the movements of our patrols for a couple of days, familiarize themselves with the terrain and then launch an infiltration. However, the actual terrorist camps are a few kilometres inside. Here, the element of surprise was absolutely crucial to the outcome. Since our commandos were walking well inside enemy territory, they walked like ghosts so that, paradoxically, they could stay alive to fight.

The trickiest part was passing through their forward line of defence. Forward defences (group of posts) on both sides are protected by minefields. Landmines are buried in the ground to deter the attacker or infiltrator. They also tend to get dislodged by snowfall and rain. It is these that cause maximum damage because their location is unknown.

On possible infiltration routes, trip flares are fixed which light up when touched and illuminate the infiltrator for half a minute. Night-vision-enabled equipment was also used at the posts to keep a vigil round the clock on likely routes of infiltration. And to make things worse, the soldiers manning the posts would let off a round of bullets now and then as deterrence. The commandos had to cross all these dangers and hurdles without being detected.

What helped us was the fact that the Pakistan Army was not prepared for infiltration because they didn't expect us to be carrying out any such manoeuvres. While the Indian side is trained to deal with infiltrators, and thus deploy ambush parties and use other such measures, the Pakistani side are a little more static and focus more on manning the LoC posts. It gives me great satisfaction to observe that from 2016 they have also had to deploy soldiers to guard against a possible repeat of our surgical strike. The 'uncertainty' mode has been switched on.

The tension mounted in the early hours of 29 September 2016. We were to start the raids simultaneously after everyone was in position. Suddenly I was told that firing had started in one of the locations. I wasn't sure if our team had been discovered and the enemy had fired first or one of our teams had started the firing for whatever reason. Since the first shot had been fired, we decided to advance the launch by fifteen–twenty minutes.

Now that the raids had begun, the anxiety in the operations room ratcheted – would this turn out to be a calculated risk or a reckless gamble? Would we achieve success in the mission? What if there were heavy casualties? There were moments when I found myself extremely confident that all would be well. I had taken a leap of faith, and I believe fortune favours the brave. Then the next moment I would find myself on pins and needles, thinking of everything that could possibly go wrong.

This was the first time I realized how difficult it is for someone who has been in operations to sit outside and control it. First, you miss the action and you want to be there in the middle of it – participating and directing. Second, sitting outside, far away in an operations room yet intimately involved in each and every step of the planning, you feel utterly powerless. Thank heavens my vacillating moods could not be seen by the brave soldiers conducting the operations.

At one of the terrorist camps, we got lucky. A huge petrol and diesel dump was hit by a handheld rocket launcher and caused heavy casualties. The explosion created a huge blast which could even be seen in the UAV footage. Although the blast could not be heard, the black cloud of smoke that rose in the air obliterated our view of the drone footage. It seemed a fitting response to the fire that had engulfed the cookhouse and tents at Uri.

The strikes on terrorist camps across the LoC did not last very long. Ours was a swift operation conducted with precision, and while there was the temptation to stay on and cause more damage, the team leaders, as they had rehearsed, broke contact and withdrew rapidly so that they could easily escape back to our side of the LoC. Dawn was breaking.

Now was the crucial period of the whole operation – from the moment the soldiers began to exfiltrate to our side till the point the last man came back in. This is the period when the soldier has neither the element of surprise nor darkness to defend himself. Our anxiety in the control room reached a fever pitch at this point. Every time the phone rang, I would flinch, half expecting news of some casualty. At least to me, my sigh of relief was very audible every time it turned out to be some other news. And thankfully, it always was.

Within thirty minutes, our men were all back on the Indian side of the LoC. Not a single soldier had been injured during the raid. When I reported to the Army Commander that the operation had been successful and that all our soldiers were back safely, I could sense his relief across the line. We could feel this with whoever we spoke to on the phone after the mission, up or down the chain.

Army Headquarters had been informed. The leadership had been apprised by the Army Chief. Lieutenant General Ranbir Singh, Director General Military Operations (DGMO), told his counterpart in Pakistan over the telephone that the Indian Army had hit terrorist camps across the LoC because of the terror attack at Uri where we had lost eighteen soldiers. He also told him that we had no desire to escalate this any further. He was essentially saying that the ball was in Pakistan's court – if they wished to expand the conflict, the onus would be on them.

Surgical Strike Across the LoC

By mid-morning, the DGMO was ready to make a press statement and answer questions. The national media had been assembled, news had started trickling out and there was excitement in the whole country at the stupendous success of what came to be known as the surgical strike.

I spoke with the DGMO and told him to hold off the announcement till we took a full headcount of all soldiers returning after the ops. Everyone in Delhi wanted to start the press conference, but I insisted that we wait till we could confirm that every single one of our soldiers was back safely. This would have delayed them by about an hour. But it meant that we could announce that we had inflicted heavy casualties on the terrorists in their camps across the LoC for the first time and not incurred a single casualty of our own. As I said, fortune favours the brave.

It was around noon, if my memory serves me right, when the DGMO announced to the world that we had hit terrorist camps across the LoC. He also announced that we had no desire to escalate the situation, and that the Pakistan DGMO had also been told this over the telephone.

The media used the term 'surgical strike', and the name stuck. It merits mention here that while there have been shallow operations across the LoC in the past from both sides, what was different this time was the scale and the depth of the targets. And the fact that we owned up to it proactively. It was also for the first time that we used diplomacy as leverage for an operation. We had, for example, built public opinion against the terrorist strikes at Uri by using the UN General Assembly as a forum.

Soon after the press conference, the team leaders were flown in by helicopter to my headquarters for a quick debrief. I could see that they were exhausted, but their faces were glowing, their body language was jubilant. When they saluted me and said 'Jai Hind, sir', I was filled with emotion. I returned their salute crisply and said, 'Thank you, boys. Thank God you have all come back safe and sound. History will remember you for what you have achieved today.'

And then, before they could start discussing the operation, the boy who used to bring us tea entered with a tray. As instructed by me, instead of tea, the tray held a few bottles of Johnnie Walker Black Label. 'Normally this would be the time for beer, but today is not a normal day. It's not a day for beer; these tigers need something stronger.' That drew a lot of laughter. Everyone was in high spirits.

I then turned towards Brigadier Rana Kalita, Brigadier General Staff (BGS), and said, 'These SF guys are in the habit of eating whisky glasses, so I'm not going to risk it.' With that, I opened a bottle of Black Label myself and poured a decent slug into their mouths one by one. You know all about having a shot of whisky. Well, these guys were getting shot by whisky.

Then one of them took the bottle and said,

'Permission to give a shot to the Corps Commander, sir.' I opened my mouth and he poured in a generous measure. I thought I would get a kick and feel high after drinking straight from the bottle. But I was already on a high and so, I suspect, were all of them. I also realized that they must be really tired and the adrenaline rush couldn't carry them forever, so we rushed through a quick debrief and did a more detailed one the next day.

I received a phone call at around 3.30 p.m. 'Sir, the defence minister wants to talk to you.' His private secretary came on the line first and congratulated me. When the defence minister came on the line, he said only one word, 'Congratulations.' It was a little disconcerting as he didn't say anything more. I replied, 'Jai Hind, sir, congratulations to you too. Sir, this is your victory as much as of the soldiers who went across. Thank you for giving us the go-ahead to conduct this operation.' He replied, 'Yes, I'm glad that all our soldiers are safe. Thank you again.'

Surgical Strike Across the LoC

It was a stupendous operation, something that had never been done before. We had struck at terrorist camps across the LoC and eliminated a large number of terrorists. This surgical strike, in effect, set the stage for the Balakot air strikes when the terrorist attack happened at Pulwama a year and a half later. We had drawn new red lines and India had shed the soft-state tag. I had never imagined that I would get an opportunity to be capping nearly four decades of my service with a glorious operation like this.

One cannot overcome the grief of the loss of eighteen soldiers in Uri, but the surgical strike gave us a sense of closure. I salute the memory of the departed, and I salute the bravery of the bravehearts who executed the surgical strike.

Secrecy is the key to any successful operation. If you catch the enemy unawares, half your battle has been won.

2

Leading from the Front

It's the ultimate dream of an infantry officer to command his own battalion, which is the unit he is commissioned in, and get an opportunity to lead his men in war. When I was promoted to the rank of Colonel, I became the CO of my own unit, a Param Vir Chakra (PVC) Battalion, with a rich history of honours and awards to its credit. It was a dream come true.

A battalion has about a thousand soldiers. Three battalions make a brigade, and three brigades are organized into a division. Three divisions are grouped in a corps. In the army, a battalion is the basic unit. A unit or battalion is also colloquially called paltan.

I took over the command of the battalion just as we were sent into a part of the LoC in J&K. This was a very 'hot' area, with lots of terrorists, cross-border firing and infiltration attempts. Within the first week we had our first encounter with terrorists, and I lost an officer.

We received an intelligence report that three terrorists had taken shelter in a village house across the river, just a couple of kilometres from the Battalion Headquarters. Major Rohit Sharma, who received the report, was the only officer present at the base at that moment. He swung the Quick Reaction Team (QRT) into action, leading them himself, and asked for extra reinforcements to follow. The commando platoon called Ghatak, deployed a few kilometres away, was ordered to reach at the earliest the village where the terrorists were said to have taken shelter.

Major Rohit Sharma was a very smart, capable and brave officer. A handsome young six-footer from Punjab, he was an athlete, a keen sportsman with a very pleasant personality. His troops loved him, his junior officers adored him and I found him a very reliable member of the team.

His team crept up to the house in which the terrorists were hiding and laid a cordon around it. They also occupied the neighbouring two-storeyed house which was about thirty metres away. There were terraced fields all around.

After the cordon was in place, he personally led the assault team and sneaked up to the target house, using the fire-and-move tactic, where a few soldiers move at a time, while the others keep the enemy engaged. The terrorists started lobbing grenades and firing at them with AK rifles. The assault team retaliated in kind and took up position behind a half-constructed mud wall and a tree. Some of our team took up a firing-cum-observation post in a house nearby, while others took position in the shelter of the next level of the terraced field.

This exchange of fire continued, with neither side managing a breakthrough. Rohit observed some movement in the window from where the terrorists were firing. He crawled forward and, at grave risk to his life, lobbed a hand grenade through the window. The grenade seemed to have met its mark and loud cries were heard.

Rohit's brave action proved to be a turning point in the fight. Eventually, after a prolonged exchange of firing, one terrorist tried to break through the cordon. Despite the dust and smoke, Rohit quickly intercepted him and fired at him at point-blank range. But during the close combat encounter, he was also hit at close range by the terrorist's bullets. At the end of it, while all three terrorists were killed, Rohit too paid with his life.

I was overcome with grief. I had arrived midway into the encounter and witnessed Rohit's death. The loss of a young Major and a good friend in front of my eyes was a massive blow, professionally and personally. This was the first death I had to face as CO. There were many more to come later in my life, but that day I felt my world had come crashing down.

How would I face Rohit's family? How would I face my unit in which I had served and grown over the last twenty years? My own career was surely over. These were the thoughts that plagued me. I just couldn't sleep that night.

I tossed and turned, my mind unable to rest. Then the training and discipline of the army kicked in, and I started to think like a professionally trained army officer, like a Commanding Officer. As dawn broke, I came to the realization that Rohit's sacrifice had not been in vain. This brave officer had killed three terrorists; not a single one had escaped. Isn't that a combat soldier's ultimate purpose in life? He was a hero. So many heroic deeds in the world were also tragedies. Lives had to be given up to accomplish great things.

So the next morning I gathered my soldiers and spoke to them. 'Yesterday we lost a brave officer who took a bullet in his chest while leading from the front, but all the three terrorists were eliminated. His bravery also saved the lives of some of our soldiers. He is a hero.'

Recalling our past battles and victories fires up the fighting spirit of soldiers and lifts their morale, all the more so after they have suffered the loss of a comrade. So I went on to remind them, 'Our battalion has had such a rich history of gallantry in all our operations since Independence. Look at what we did in the Siachen Glacier a decade ago. There too our first casualty was an officer. Remember how we covered ourselves in glory after that, executing the attack at the highest altitude in the world, capturing Bana Top, winning a Param Vir Chakra, a Mahavir Chakra and a host of other awards. We are going to do that again. What is the best way to pay homage to Major Rohit Sharma?

By ensuring that not a single terrorist remains in our area.'

Rohit's death so early in my time as CO shaped many of my decisions. I was determined that our battalion make its mark, and we went on to eliminate 106 terrorists/enemies during my three years as CO of the battalion, which is a record of sorts in J&K till date.

In our next encounter with terrorists, I didn't wear a bulletproof jacket – I was acting braver than I felt. I also did not carry a weapon. When my team insisted, I told them that my job was to plan. If I had an AK rifle in my hands, I would be tempted to get drawn into firing. It would distract me from my main task of planning the operation and thinking ahead.

My Subedar Major suggested that I carry at least a pistol for my personal security. I told him that I had full confidence in my QRT of five soldiers to protect me.

Foolhardy though it might have been, my taking this risk really inspired everyone. My QRT too were spurred to be extra careful and alert. During the encounter, I saw a very different kind of energy in my soldiers and the officers. There is just no substitute for leading from the front. Leading by setting an example is the key to leadership.

During my training at the NDA, I had read a book called *A Bridge Too Far* by Cornelius Ryan about the battle of Arnhem in World War II. In the book there was a British Major who always carried a rolled-up umbrella instead of a gun. There is a scene which depicts a German air raid in the movie based on the book. As the city gets shelled, people begin to rush to bomb shelters and trenches.

A priest also hurries down the street to seek shelter. The Major with an Umbrella, as he had by then come to be known, sees him running and calmly opens his umbrella and says, 'Come, Father, come under the umbrella!' as if it were only raining. The scene left an indelible impression on me.

Later in the book, the Major explained why he always carried an umbrella. He said that army contingents from different countries speaking different languages were fighting together at Arnhem. There was often confusion about who was friend and who was foe, and the Germans never carried umbrellas – this was a typically British habit. The Major with his umbrella had become well known by then, and saved the day for his unit several times when other Allied patrols recognized them as British because of that umbrella.

A friend and I often used to discuss the Major's attitude and were very impressed by it. Now as a CO in a combat situation, I started practising my own version of the Major's tactic.

In those three years I decided never to wear a bulletproof jacket or bulletproof patka (which provided helmet-like protection). I used to wear a floppy hat made of camouflage uniform fabric, instead of the Cap FS that was worn by all soldiers and officers. I also wore two more badges, which were not common, on my uniform. One was a parachute badge, as I had done five basic parachute jumps voluntarily. The second was a badge with a commando dagger that all those who had been commando instructors were entitled to wear. The parachute badge was white and sky blue in colour, and the commando badge was red. Both are worn on the front right shirt pocket according to the dress regulations.

These brightly coloured badges along with the floppy hat were so distinctive that all the officers and soldiers of my battalion could recognize their CO from a kilometre or more away – it is possible to see that far on mountain slopes or across rivers and valleys in that area.

Like the officer with the umbrella, these badges that I insisted on wearing saved my life and my QRT's too during an operation. On a dark, moonless night, one of our ambush parties close to the LoC spotted a group of infiltrating terrorists. The ambush party consisted of only four soldiers, so it would not have been prudent for them to tackle the terrorists themselves. They alerted the Company Commander on the radio set, who ordered them to lie still, let the terrorists pass and follow them stealthily from a distance till they came to a particular area in a narrow valley. The Company Commander would move there with strong reinforcements to trap the terrorists in what is known in army parlance as the killing ground.

It was important that the ambush party keep the infiltrating group in sight without giving them any clue that they were on to them. When Major Himanshu Sawant, the Company Commander, informed me of the plan, two more platoons were moved from the headquarters to form another interception line, beyond the next ridgeline, between their position and the Battalion Headquarters, just in case the terrorists escaped from the encounter site.

The small team that was tailing the terrorists held the key to the success of this operation. Shadow patrolling is one of the trickiest manoeuvres for soldiers – to tail from a distance, but not alert the target, especially on a dark night with very little visibility, is extremely hard. We were very hopeful of a successful operation and waited with bated breath.

But alas, before they could reach the killing ground, there was an extremely heavy shower with thunder and lightning. Bad weather is the perfect time for terrorists to infiltrate, and despite our best efforts, we lost visual contact with them.

We were disappointed, but we waited in the rain nonetheless. I had walked up with the two additional platoons that we had sent up from the Battalion Headquarters, each under an officer. We were all sopping wet. I took position under a tree with my QRT. But a tree only delays the effect of rain by a few minutes. Oh boy, did it pour that night!

As day broke, I realized that waiting was futile.

So I called off the operation and we walked back to the base. It took us over an hour and we were tired, wet and chilled to the bone, frustrated and disappointed.

As I reached the base, I decided to debrief the different parties before we changed out of our wet uniforms. Major Himanshu Sawant's party would arrive a little later because they had a longer distance to cover. I decided that I would hear them out separately later.

After we finished, I sent the others away to change and sat down on the lawn of the officers' mess for a cup of tea. My buddy brought me a spare pair of boots from my room. Soldiers operate within a buddy system – always two together. An officer's buddy is a young soldier who marks his map, draws his weapon and ammunition and provides necessary assistance. I decided to change out of my wet boots while waiting for Himanshu and the hot cup of tea. For those who have never experienced it, it is incredibly difficult to take off wet jungle boots. An operation in itself!

The Adjutant, Major Sean O'Brien, was enjoying my plight and teasing me. During operations, soldiers drop all formalities. The soles of my feet were shrivelled, having been soaked all night. I was enjoying the sensation of rubbing the soles of my feet on the grass before putting on dry boots. The tea showed up just then, and the steaming cup added to my feeling of well-being. Dry shoes, a hot cup of tea, the small pleasures of life.

The joy was short-lived. I must have taken just a couple of sips when suddenly I heard a burst of automatic fire – it was more than one AK rifle. A soldier came running and shouted, '*Sir, Himanshu sahab ki team ka taakra ho gaya hai, nale mein* (Major Himanshu's team has made contact with the terrorists in the nala).'

Major Himanshu's party were on their way back to the base when an informant told them that the terrorists we were tailing last night had sought refuge in a gharat or watermill in the Mandi riverbed, less than a kilometre from our base.

I dispatched a few teams to cover all possible escape routes, hurriedly pulled on my dry boots and rushed out to meet my QRT, my uniform still half wet. Almost all of them were wet from the previous night's outing, but live combat spurs the spirits.

Just then I realized that I had not sent any team across the river to cut off the terrorists in case they managed to cross it. There were three or four water channels in the riverbed, and in some stretches it was possible to make a crossing. So I decided that I would go across with my QRT. If we climbed to a little height, it would also enable me to get a bird's-eye view of the whole operation from the other side of the river.

We had to cross a fifty-metre-long rope suspension bridge to get to the other bank of the Mandi river. There was obviously no cover. The encounter had started in the gharat which was on our side of the water channel, so the bullets were flying close by.

Normally you walk slowly, one person at a time, on a suspension bridge because it swings with each step. We ran across the bridge one after the other to minimize exposure to bullets. As we ran, I thought it would be quite funny if one of us slipped and fell into the river. The risk of that happening was high, as was the risk of getting hit by a bullet. How much wetter could a wet man get? But my shoes would be wet again, I thought wryly!

Once we were safely across the river, we proceeded towards the gharat from the other side of the river. The firing intensified at the watermill. I could see two huts there. A couple of grenades were also lobbed by both sides. Suddenly we heard the wails of a woman over the noise of the water and the firing. We found a middle-aged woman who had been shot in the knee by a stray bullet.

She was accompanied by her teenage daughter, who had tied a piece of her dupatta around her mother's knee to stop the bleeding. The lady was bleeding profusely and wailing loudly. We bandaged her wound with a dressing from our first aid kit, but her condition was bad. I tried to console her, and told one of my boys to carry her so that we could get her to a hospital fast.

We tried to message for help, but the radio batteries were dead. The spare battery also didn't work as it was completely soaked. Another unexpected problem arose – the woman refused to be carried by a man. I shouted at her good-naturedly, '*Mai, jaan bachani hai toh sharam mat kar. Bahut khoon beh gaya hai. Yeh tere bete jaisa hai* (If you want to save yourself, stop feeling shy and let this boy carry you. You've already lost a lot of blood. He is like your son).'

Thereafter, our progress was slowed because of her. The good news was that the firing was petering out. The bad news was that we could not get in touch with anyone on the radio set. We had two sets, but no live batteries. After some time we could even see the movement of our soldiers across the river on the encounter site. All appeared well till suddenly a few shots were fired at us from behind, from a height.

We dashed and took cover in the hollows and rocks in the riverbed. The firing stopped. We could not spot any activity. After five minutes we moved again cautiously. We had walked barely fifteen metres when we were fired upon again. We took cover. One of my soldiers noticed some movement on top of the ridgeline some distance away.

I remembered that Major Deshpande's party was on the ridgeline in the south to cut off any fleeing terrorists. They were shooting at us thinking we were escaping terrorists. We tried to call them on radio, hoping against hope that we might get through, but in vain. After five to seven minutes, we again started moving carefully, creeping and crawling towards the roadhead.

It was a funny situation. The encounter with the terrorists seemed to have ended. We had a civilian casualty on our hands, and our own troops were firing at us. We could not communicate with each other. What if Himanshu's party started firing at us from the other side to support Deshpande's effort? Then we would be in a seriously dangerous situation.

But thankfully they didn't, because, as I learnt later, they knew that they had killed all three terrorists. We had crawled only about fifty metres when we were fired upon again. One bullet landed very close to my foot and I thought I felt a small stone splinter on my face as it ricocheted off the rocks.

Maybe it was the splinter, maybe it was the wet clothes, maybe it was the lack of sleep, maybe the woman bleeding profusely who needed medical attention urgently, or maybe it was all of these put together that made me do what I did next.

I got up, stood erect, adjusted my floppy hat and took a few steps forward, saying to my QRT that our boys would recognize their CO. I walked slowly. There was no more firing. Major Manoj Deshpande later told me that they could make out their CO and his misshapen floppy camouflage hat, and a closer look with his binoculars showed him the parachute wing and commando badge.

My QRT boys stood up and joined me, and we reached the road in a few minutes. We sent the wounded woman to the doctor, and were happy to learn that all three terrorists had been eliminated and all our boys were safe and unhurt.

That we came very close to being hit because of mistaken identity was something we all sat and talked about over and over again, and still do. My floppy hat and badges are always the punchline. Anything that saves a soldier's life becomes part of his folklore. This became mine.

There is just no substitute for leading from the front. Leading by setting an example is the key to leadership.

3
Life on the LoC

The LoC is a world apart, with a life of its own. It is a roughly 750-kilometre-long unresolved border between India and Pakistan in J&K and Ladakh. As the name suggests, the dynamic here is of 'grabbers keepers'.

It was this that led to the Kargil war in 1999. The Pakistan Army infiltrated the LoC and illegally occupied several mountain peaks in Kargil. The Indian Army had to launch Operation Vijay to evict them. The summer of 1999 was the summer of valour. The war was led largely by junior leaders, the twenty-something young officers who battled against the odds with ferocity and passion, many giving up their lives. They were an inspiration to the Indian Army and the whole country.

We lost over 500 brave soldiers and officers, but not even an inch of our territory. Fortunately, Operation Vijay remained confined to the LoC. It did not spill over into the international borders. What is the difference between the two, one may ask.

An international border is accepted and ratified by the parliaments or equivalents of both countries. The LoC, on the other hand, is exactly as the name suggests. So you have to man it, that is, sit on it physically, to control your area. Incidentally, in army parlance it is called LC and not LoC as it is more commonly known.

Similarly, most of the India–China border is an unresolved border called LAC – Line of Actual Control – which is nearly 3500 kilometres long. It was agreed to after the India–China war of 1962. Here too both countries have differing perceptions of the border. Several rounds of talks between the two countries have failed to resolve the issue.

Although historically it has not been as volatile and violent as the LoC, the LAC also heats up at times. For several years we had only occasional face-offs between the two armies. However, the most recent one at Ladakh in the spring of 2020, when after nearly half a century both sides suffered fatal casualties, may well be a turning point.

The LoC usually runs along a defined feature like a nala (mountain stream), a ridgeline or a mountain spur, but at times it cuts across features and even villages. The steep mountainsides are full of terraced fields in these border villages and are very picturesque when the standing crop is lush. However, they are also prone to infiltration because the fields go right up to the LoC, and people have relatives across the line.

Since it does not have any fence or markers, the army occupies posts on the high mountain peaks so that it can keep guard over the larger area on which it sits. Pakistan has a similar set of posts right opposite ours. It is at these posts that fire is exchanged, and it is through the gaps between these posts that the other side infiltrates terrorists. It may take anything up to a couple of hours to walk to the next post, which may well be on the next mountain peak. Two adjacent posts man the area in between.

Each post has a number of bunkers. A bunker is a very small room, most of it underground, which offers protection against enemy fire, and has loopholes from where our soldiers can fire their weapons at the enemy. Its walls and roof are extremely thick so it can absorb artillery shelling and rocket attacks.

Soldiers deployed on a post live there permanently. They sleep and fight there, train and cook there, maintain their weapons and are stocked with ammunition, food and other stores that they might need. It is a special kind of community living.

Some of these posts are in very high reaches

which get snowbound in the winter. Patrols are sent from these posts to connect with neighbouring posts or the area around. Such patrols run the risk of being fired upon by the enemy or washed away by avalanches. Life on the posts is exciting but it can get to a soldier if he has a prolonged stay there, so we try and send the soldiers on leave after two to three months.

Today the LoC is a violent place, but it wasn't always like this. In the early 1980s, when my unit was deployed in Kupwara in north Kashmir, life on the LoC was fairly peaceful. There was no infiltration and almost no firing across it. In fact, we would even occasionally interact with soldiers on the opposite side, especially when locals approached us because their cattle had strayed across.

The Pakistani soldiers would call out to us asking for sugar, as they used to get gur in their tea rations. Once when I was Captain, we yelled out an Eid Mubarak greeting to a Pakistan Army Junior

Commissioned Officer (JCO) on the opposite post.

He asked us, '*Sahab, agar main aapko sewaiyan doon toh aap khayenge? Haan, main aapke saamne usmein se do chammach kha loonga* (If I give you sweetened wheat noodles [the traditional sweet dish prepared on Eid], will you eat it? I will eat a bit out of that bowl in front of you [implying that it was not laced with poison or anything harmful].'

Major Yashpal Singh, who was the Post Commander, warmly replied that we would eat it happily without his having to prove that it was safe. Military to military, we are brothers-at-arms, and not surprisingly, we find it easy to talk to each other.

In 1999, my battalion was also deployed on the LoC, albeit not in Kargil but in another part of the LoC in J&K. By then there was a lot of activity on the LoC – frequent firing as well as infiltration attempts by terrorists, heightened by the tensions of the Kargil war.

In those days, I used to spend my days in

different company locations on the forward posts of the LoC. One day I went to visit one of the forward platoons, from where the enemy post was just fifty metres away. The LoC ran between these two posts. I spent some time at the post, reviewing the defence preparedness and chatting with the boys over the ubiquitous chai and pakoras.

I was pleased to see that the soldiers on the post were enthusiastic about their work, and their morale and motivation levels were high. I then went into the Post Commander's bunker to change out of my uniform into a set of civvies, as did my QRT soldiers.

On the forward slopes, that is, any slope that descends towards the enemy, where one was exposed to enemy view and fire, we normally did not move in uniform. Instead, we dressed in a Pathan suit which is worn by the locals and which was convenient to walk, although not to run, in. If you threw on a bukkal (shawl) like the locals did, the soldiers could hide their weapons as well.

The LoC in this part runs along a big nala. The slope on our side was a forward slope which went down to the nala. The slope that rose from the other side of the nala was in Pakistan-Occupied Kashmir (PoK). The mountainside was covered with terraced fields, as is the case with cultivable land in the mountains. There were very few trees which could provide cover from the enemy.

By wearing local attire it was easy to mingle with the villagers who were working in the fields on the forward slopes. The Pakistan Army would not fire at the locals, lest they run the risk of losing their support during the infiltration of terrorists.

It was going to turn dark in an hour or so, and we would take about two hours to reach the roadhead from where I would drive back to my battalion base. We had barely walked thirty or forty metres from the post when Subedar Bal Raj, the Post Commander, asked us to halt.

He said that the Pakistani soldiers on the

opposite post had yelled out to him, saying, 'Your men are walking fully exposed on forward slopes. Please ask them to stop, otherwise we will be forced to open fire.'

I shouted back to him, asking him to tell them that none of our soldiers were outside, that he was mistaken and the men must be local villagers. They replied, 'We even know it's your CO. Please don't continue this movement or else you will be responsible for the consequences. Our Company Commander has given strict orders.'

It dawned on me then that owing to heightened firing across the LoC during Operation Vijay, not many locals were moving about on the forward slopes. Since the Pakistani post was so close, they must have observed my activities as I had reviewed the security of our post. But I also wondered if I should listen to their threat and give them the satisfaction of having scared the CO of the Indian battalion.

Life on the LoC is a lot about psychological

domination and aggressive behaviour. I thought for a bit and told Subedar Bal Raj to climb to the observation tower post where a sentry always stood guard to keep a lookout. It was from the observation post just across ours that the Pakistanis had shouted their warning.

It was clear that they too were playing mind games and did not want to escalate the LoC firing situation, otherwise they would have fired instead of giving a warning. Our posts dominated theirs in this area, and we could cause serious damage and casualties to them with our heavy weapons if we had to.

Once the Post Commander was in visual contact with the Pakistan sentry, I asked him to relay to the sentry whatever I told him. He did. This is the gist of what he shouted across the LoC.

'If you start firing on our CO's party, I doubt the first bullet will hit the CO. But as soon as the first shot is fired, I guarantee you that your post will be flattened. We will use all possible weapons and rockets. Your post is surrounded by three of ours. You will be responsible for the casualties that you incur.'

I waited for five minutes for the message to reach their Company Commander. Then I asked my team if we should move ahead. *'Darein ya chalein?'* Unanimously, they chose to march ahead.

Cautiously, we stepped forward. About five minutes of walking brought us out in the open. For the next twenty minutes of our walk, we would be completely exposed to the enemy's view, which meant we would be at his mercy. Should he choose to fire at us, we would be sitting ducks.

What if they opened fire on us and we did have heavy casualties? I started having doubts – why did I take this step? Had I been too arrogant? There were very few trees, mostly open terraced fields.

We would have no natural cover if firing broke out. Every step was a step taken in suspense, the air felt heavier than usual and there was silence among us. The tension only ended once we reached the tree cover of the next post.

I heaved a sigh of relief. We were really living on the edge on the LoC, I thought to myself. We were bearing the brunt of some of the not-so-sound decisions taken in the past. We defended with our lives the lines drawn by someone on a map.

As I mentioned earlier, we lived by the ethos of 'grabbers keepers', playing mind games to remain dominant at all costs, often at grave risk to life.

If they had fired that day and caused casualties, anyone would have been right to comment, 'What did you achieve? You took the lives of your own soldiers,' that is, if I was not the one to be killed. But any soldier who has operated on the LoC would do the same thing.

This was the constantly tension-charged atmosphere on the LoC. And to think that most of our countrymen feel that soldiers just stand idle on sentry duty there, like the watchman they see at the gate of their building or outside a bank.

⌜ We were really living on the edge on the LoC. We were bearing the brunt of some not-so-sound decisions taken in the past. We defended with our lives the lines drawn by someone else on a map. ⌟

4
Main aur Meri Helmet

One morning the Subedar Major came running to my office saying that two villagers had come from a nearby village with the news that six terrorists had forcibly taken shelter in the house of a relative of theirs. The terrorists looked tired, and while they were resting, a boy from the household had slipped out to inform us.

The village was about an hour's walk from our base, which was on the bank of the Mandi river. There were very few villages and a relatively sparse population between the LoC and the river. When terrorists infiltrated, they aimed to get across the Mandi to the more densely populated side where they would be able to merge more easily with the locals.

The entire area between the LoC and the river was our responsibility, and all my companies and the other smaller detachments such as the Ghatak Platoon and logistics units were tactically deployed at various points in this vast area. It was my mandate to ensure that no infiltrator was able to get across the river.

It so happened that I was the only officer present at the battalion base when we received information about the six terrorists hiding in the nearby village. My Adjutant, the officer who would have led the operation, happened to be away. He doubled up as the Quartermaster, looking after logistics, and had gone to the Brigade Headquarters in the morning for a logistics conference. Two other search operations had been launched earlier that morning and it would take some time for those troops to be diverted back. So I decided to go ahead and lead the operation personally till the backup platoon under Major Himanshu Sawant reached the village where the terrorists were holed up.

Here I must also explain that for every operation that turned into a successful encounter, we would carry out eight to ten search operations that didn't pan out. Most of the tip-offs we received would prove to be wrong or outdated, or both. That day, however, I felt confident that the information was correct and current, because these two men were not our usual sources who brought second-hand information. They were relatives of the man into whose house the terrorists had forced their way in.

I got the necessary strength of soldiers ready to launch the operation even as Himanshu's platoon from the LoC was summoned. His party would reach later because they were located further away from the village. However, they would have to walk downhill while my party had to walk uphill from the base.

As we were about to start from the base, I saw the Subedar Major briefing my QRT members very intently. A Subedar Major is the seniormost enlisted soldier of the battalion. He is a very respected father figure for all the soldiers. Around ten years older than the CO, a good Subedar Major is his right-hand man. He marries his experience and wisdom while expressing his opinion and advising senior officers, not hesitating to advise even the CO.

I jokingly said to him, '*Kya ho gaya, sahab, aaj meri QRT se bahut baatein ho rahi hain?* (What's the matter, today you're having very long discussions with my Quick Reaction Team)?' He said, 'Sir, this is the first time that you are going not only as the CO, but also as the officer in charge of this team.' I was very pleased by his reply; this is the kind of stabilizing role that a Subedar Major is supposed to play in a battalion.

He also reminded me that I had to make a brief visit to the unit temple before setting out for the operation. I followed his advice and sought the blessings of the Almighty.

We walked through the villages and fields until we came to a rocky slope with very few fields and buildings. There were only a small number of scattered houses, beyond which one could see the barren slopes leading up to the ridgeline.

A cluster of three houses was pointed out to me in which the terrorists were said to be resting. They had been walking for a couple of days to reach their destination and were exhausted. They had asked for food and then gone off to sleep. They would not be in one house, so we had to plan on laying a cordon to cover all three houses.

I asked both the platoons to fan out and establish a cordon among the rocks and trees that dotted the landscape. It was a treat to see the soldiers harmoniously move under cover just as they had been instructed, despite the fact that they did not belong to a single platoon or company. I had pulled together all the soldiers who were at the base for any reason, including those waiting to go on leave or to the hospital the next day. It took about thirty minutes for the cordon to be established.

The Cordon Commander, Subedar Karnail Singh, gave me the completion report on the radio along with another piece of good news – Major Himanshu's platoon would also arrive in another half-hour or so. He was to arrive from the north, walking downwards, while my party which had fanned out into a cordon would now silently move uphill from the south. The aim was to completely encircle the enemy.

My platoon started moving upwards carefully. If you don't follow a track, walking up the terraced fields is not easy. After every twenty to thirty metres, you have to climb up to the next terrace. It was like climbing a mud wall which was five to ten feet high.

Suddenly AK rifles began to be fired from one of the houses. Everyone ducked and took cover below the mud walls of the fields. Once I had established that no one was hit, the feeling that overcame me was paradoxically one of excitement and relief. I felt happy that our information about the terrorists was correct and that the cordon was in place. We were ready for a successful operation.

We were at a slight disadvantage, however, as they were firing downhill at us, which is always more effective, while our range of movement was restricted. Whenever my boys tried to fire back, the terrorists would fire from within the house and we had to duck as we were in the open. In fact, their bullets were hitting very close to my feet. I remember curling up my feet and seeing the dust rise from the bullets that fell near me.

After a few minutes of being pinned under fire, we received some good news. My radio operator informed me that Himanshu's party had reached and they had opened fire on the terrorists uphill from the house. This forced the terrorists to split their attention and give us a bit of a breather.

We decided to crawl to the other side of a dry nala about forty metres away and position ourselves behind a cluster of rocks. It would allow us to get closer to the houses and give us a better position.

As I was about to get up, a member of my QRT, Rifleman Sher Singh, blocked my way and insisted that I wear a helmet. He held out an extra helmet to me. I told him, 'You know that I don't wear a helmet; I have never worn a helmet in operations.' He was unmoved, '*Sahab, abhi bilkul kargar fire hai aur range bhi bahut kam hai* (The terrorists' fire is very effective and from a very close range).'

He requested again that I wear the helmet. I tried to make light of it, 'Come on, Sher Singh, let's go, *kuchh nahin hoga* (nothing will happen).' But he would not let me go past him. He then said something that touched me. 'Subedar Major sahab will court-martial me – that is what he was telling me before we left. He told me that if there was a situation where I saw you risking your life, it was my duty to save you. He specially told me to insist that you wear your helmet.'

The Subedar Major's impassioned briefing flashed before my eyes. I was overwhelmed. I took the helmet from Sher Singh and wore it for the one rare time during these operations.

That day we went on to eliminate those six dreaded terrorists and recovered a large quantity of arms and ammunition. It was one of our most successful operations. My biggest happiness was that all our soldiers were safe. But there are a couple of interesting side stories to tell, and they have to do with helmets.

At one stage during the operation, we had shot down three of the terrorists in one of the houses. The other three who were in the second house made a break for it and started running up the slope through the rocks.

These terrorists were wearing combat jackets and it was difficult to make out the difference between our soldiers and the terrorists from a distance.

Sitting on my rocky vantage point, a solution struck me like a flash. I took the radio set from my radio operator and said, 'All stations, Tiger here. All soldiers must wear helmets. Terrorists are wearing combat jackets, but not helmets. Anyone not wearing a helmet, shoot him down.' And that is what our soldiers did. The last terrorist had surprisingly reached quite far through the rocks when he was brought down.

There's another unbelievable twist. Naib Subedar Karnail Singh brought Rifleman Kamal Deep from one of the assault teams to me as we were winding up and checking our weapons and ammunition. He said, 'Sir, you won't believe this!' He showed me a bullet hole in front of Kamal's helmet right in the centre, just a little above the forehead. Then he showed me the exit hole at the back of the helmet.

A bullet had penetrated his helmet a little above the forehead and exited from behind, travelling through the couple of inches of space between the

Main aur Meri Helmet

helmet and the head. I was stunned that Kamal was still alive.

'Were you really wearing this helmet?' I asked in disbelief. 'Did you feel the bullet hitting your helmet, Kamal?' He was visibly dazed with relief at his miraculous escape from death but simply replied, 'No, sir. I thought some mud and stone ricochet had hit my helmet since bullets were landing on the ground close to me.' How lucky can a man get! What a close shave!

Luck was on our side that day, from receiving sudden information from an unexpected quarter to getting timely support from Major Himanshu's company. The many things that could have gone wrong worked out right for us that day. Fortune favours the brave! But playing it safe and wearing a helmet does help!

⌐A Subedar Major is the seniormost enlisted soldier of the battalion. He is a very respected father figure for all the soldiers, and the right-hand man of the CO.⌐

5

That Was Close!

When a soldier goes into battle, he knows he may not return, or that his battle wounds may cripple him for life. He operates under the concept of unlimited liability. But he has no time to think about such things. He cannot fear for his life, he cannot think about his family or children. He thinks only about the success of the mission.

In a soldier's world, the line between life and death is always a thin one. Every day can be a day when he has missed death. In fact, a soldier usually doesn't even notice when he has narrowly escaped death by a bullet or grenade splinter that has whizzed very close past him. Sometimes, though, he is conscious of the close shave he has had.

With a prayer of thanks, he continues to fight, without even allowing himself the luxury of feeling relief.

I, too, was fortunate a few times.

Once I was attending an operational discussion at our Brigade Headquarters in Poonch, near the LoC. All the officers who participate in these discussions are divided into syndicates that war-game the military plans.

That day we were discussing the different ways in which the enemy might attack Poonch. Poonch is the only town right on the LoC. It has its own airstrip. As we army men say, Poonch is in the show window and is regarded as a great prize by the enemy. A vulnerable town in the middle of the mountains, it had been encircled by the Pakistanis in 1947.

Midway through the discussion, the Brigade Major rushed in with the news that an encounter had broken out in my unit area. The Brigade

That Was Close!

Commander, Brigadier A.S. Sekhon, looked at me with a half-smile and said, 'I am sure you would like to go now.' I was already getting up from my seat as he was speaking. 'Best of luck,' he said as I thanked him. 'Give us the good news soon.'

My battalion was located approximately fifteen kilometres to the east of Poonch. While Poonch is a couple of kilometres from the LoC, my base was about seven to eight kilometres south of the LoC as the crow flies. Between the LoC and the base were two ridgelines of mountains, some of them as high as 9000 to 10,000 feet. My companies were deployed on these heights and occupied several posts.

Six terrorists had moved into a forested area between our base and the Ghatak Platoon post on the ridgeline. I got into my Gypsy and rushed to the area which was twenty minutes away. With me came my right-hand man, Major Himanshu Sawant, and the CO's QRT.

The CO's QRT was made up of five soldiers of the battalion who were outstanding in their fitness, firing and motivation levels. These men were my fighting buddies in all the encounters and operations for the three years that I was in command in the area.

The encounter was under way in a forested mountain slope, three kilometres short of my base. There were no mobile phones then. During the drive, I got an update from my unit base on the radio set. Apparently when the news had come in, my troops had rushed to the site.

The men from the base were sent up to lay the cordon around the target from the south. It was a huge expanse of forested mountain that took over an hour to climb. Meanwhile, the Ghatak Platoon of thirty commandos under Captain Vinod Kumar, whose camp was located higher up on the mountain, rushed down to where the terrorists were holed up.

Before the two parties could join up, the terrorists

started firing on our soldiers. We were vulnerable – we hadn't managed to encircle the encounter site fully. There were gaps in our cordon between the encounter site and the road down below to the south. If the terrorists had to make an escape downhill, they would naturally use this route that took them away from the LoC and closer to the populated centres, which was their ultimate destination.

We got to the base of the mountain and began to scale it on foot. There was a truck from my unit waiting with the driver. He had brought some ammunition from the base. However, there was nobody to carry it to the encounter site. The five men in my QRT picked up a few grenades each. They were loaded with their own weapons and ammunition and were wearing bulletproof jackets, and could not carry much else.

I was the only one who could, because I was neither carrying a weapon nor wearing a bulletproof jacket. So I picked up two pods of eighty-four millimetre rockets, each containing two rockets. These would be needed to blast through the walls behind which the terrorists were hiding. Each of these pods weighed about fifteen kilos.

Terraced fields were cut into the mountain face, and as we started walking up, the treeline got thicker, the mountain air purer. This is why sadhus came to the mountains to meditate, I would say to myself as I walked through such terrain at leisure. But that day there was no time for such reflections – it was time for action. Karma over dhyaan.

I took in the latest update from Vinod on the radio set. He asked me to put a 'stop' team on the slope that I was walking up so the terrorists would not be able to escape from that direction.

However, we did not have any men, so I detached the Light Machine Gun (LMG) Group from my QRT at a suitable spot to act as stops. This was not an advisable thing to do, as there were only four of

That Was Close!

us left now – two of my soldiers, Himanshu Sawant and I. Between us we had only three AK rifles.

As the three soldiers who were walking ahead of me had been deployed with the LMG, I now became the leading man. The first two leading soldiers in a patrol are called scouts. They keep a lookout for the enemy, one scanning the left side and the other the right. The scout also runs the risk of taking the first hit from the enemy. When one of the soldiers tried to overtake me on a narrow track to lead, I jokingly said, 'Don't worry, I can hit a terrorist with an eighty-four millimetre rocket even if I can't fire it.' It nearly came to that.

Carrying the heavy rocket pods in both hands did not make for a comfortable walk. After walking for about twenty minutes, we came to a narrow nala. It would have been hard for me to jump across carrying the pods, so instead I stretched my leg out to walk over the nala. Standing akimbo, with my legs on either side of the drain, I paused for a moment to regain my balance.

Just then I heard Himanshu shouting, 'Hey, hey, hey!' With my legs straddling either bank of the nala, I turned around to look at him.

At that moment, he started firing at me with his AK rifle. I was transfixed and shocked. Then I thought I heard a burst of rifle fire very close to my ear. When bullets fly very close to you, they produce a different and flattish sound than when you hear them from afar, and a man doesn't hear the bullet that hits him. The smell of gunpowder filled my nostrils. All of this happened in a couple of seconds. I jumped to the lower level of the terraced field, which was about eight feet below. I landed awkwardly, lost one of the rocket pods and twisted my ankle badly.

Dazed and bruised, I quickly collected myself, limped towards the mud wall and cautiously raised my head to peer over to the next level of terraced field above me where Himanshu and the boys were. The firing had been brief and had stopped after I jumped down.

That Was Close!

I saw Himanshu and two of the QRT soldiers searching the area tactically, one man crawling forward as the others covered his move, keeping a sharp lookout for any suspicious movements. I called out to him, and he crept up to me cautiously and asked if I was hurt.

He seemed almost surprised that I wasn't – a twisted ankle was not seen as an injury when you were fired at – and heaved a sigh of relief. When I told him that I had no idea what had happened and asked why he had shot at me, he almost did a double take.

It turns out that there had been a terrorist, whom I had not spotted, hiding in that nala. He must have been planning to escape down the slope towards the road, as we had anticipated. When I had paused to regain my balance while crossing the nala, he had brought out his AK rifle to take a shot at me.

Himanshu, who was about ten steps behind me (that is the distance we maintain during patrolling), spotted the terrorist below me. He shouted to alert me and immediately fired. Thank God for his presence of mind.

I was fortunate on three counts. First, that he hit the terrorist, second, that the terrorist's bullets did not hit me, and finally, that I did not get hit by a bullet from Himanshu's AK rifle, which could well have happened.

We took about ten more minutes to be reasonably sure that no more terrorists were hiding in the area. It was then that we sat down for a bit to calm ourselves. I joked with Himanshu, 'I did not feel very scared. In fact, I was more shocked than scared when you shot at me.' Himanshu replied very simply, as was his habit, 'But I was scared.' He had been scared that his bullets would hit me.

For having saved the life of the CO, Himanshu became a hero in the battalion. In fact, he became a bigger hero – he was already a star in our unit because of his exceptional bravery and quick reactions in operations. He was considered our lucky mascot. The troops felt that if he was around in an operation, we would be successful. He had proved to be our lucky charm once again.

We went on to have a successful operation that day and eliminated all six terrorists with no casualties to our side. As to one big near-miss casualty that we just spoke of, it is a story that is told again and again in our battalion. I find myself laughing the loudest when it is recounted. But I also always say a silent thanks to God and to Himanshu for saving me from death by a hair's breadth.

This wasn't my only close shave. In another encounter, we had surrounded three terrorists who were firing from a dhok, a temporary house that the villagers use during the summer season in the higher reaches of the mountains. They move there for grazing their cattle after the snow melts.

The dhok was perched on terraced fields cut into a steep mountainside and was surrounded by a thick growth of trees. This made it a hard nut to crack. The terraced fields were also planted with tall maize plants, each between six and eight feet high. This was a major problem for us as it offered effective cover to terrorists. We had to figure out a way to blast the house or smoke out the terrorists.

There was an element of urgency because it was going to become dark soon, increasing their chances of escape. I decided to move closer to the house under cover, determined to close this encounter.

Six or seven of us crawled forward on our stomachs to the next lower level of the terraced field. Our plan was to crawl close to the wall of the terrace and use the cover to approach the terrorists unobserved.

By our reckoning, only one terrorist was alive, and he was most likely low on ammunition because the encounter had gone on for a few hours already. When we were about thirty metres away, he must have detected some movement because he started firing.

He fired cautious short bursts, which confirmed that he was low on ammunition. A man low on ammunition will usually try to make a break for it sooner or later. Since we were in the lower level of the field, the bullets flew overhead. He also lobbed a couple of grenades at us.

I felt we had to wrap up the encounter soon as it was getting darker and that would give him the perfect opportunity to try to make a break for it. Suddenly I felt someone push me on my back. I turned around to see Subedar Pritam Singh (nicknamed Commando as he had been a Commando Instructor) holding on to someone with both hands in the maize field, kicking him and swearing at the top of his voice.

It took me a couple of seconds to realize that it was the terrorist who had made a dash for it through the maize crop. It was he who had pushed past me while my back was towards him. Pritam, however, had seen him and caught hold of his legs.

Since Pritam was holding on to his legs with both hands, he could not fire his weapon, so he kept kicking him in the stomach and the groin. The terrorist regained his grip over his rifle and let off a few harmless rounds as he could not turn around. The rest of my soldiers pounced on him and the terrorist was killed. It was another narrow escape. In fact, there was some blood on the back of my shirt. The terrorist must have been injured and bleeding when he pushed past me.

In another incident, I had come up to an encounter site to check things after we had killed six terrorists. Led by Subedar Bodh Raj who was in charge of the assault party, I was walking towards the two houses where the terrorists had holed themselves up. Around me our soldiers were carrying out the mandatory post-encounter tactical search of the area.

The last two terrorists had been eliminated when they had attempted to escape downhill through the trees. I could see their bodies lying about fifty metres from the house.

As I crossed Subedar Pritam and his party that was searching the area, I jokingly said, 'After so many encounters, I'm sure I don't have to list out all the precautions you need to take while approaching the dead bodies.'

There had been instances of dying terrorists creating a booby trap by keeping an open grenade between themselves and the ground so that they could cause casualties even after death. He replied confidently, 'Don't worry, sahab, we have done this several times.'

That I would grant them. The soldiers in my battalion had become very experienced and followed all the Standard Operating Procedures (SOPs) and drills diligently. When Subedar Bodh Raj and I reached the house, we stopped for a minute at the door, trying to adjust our eyes to the darkness inside.

Just then a grenade exploded nearby. Suddenly

Subedar Bodh Raj let out a loud cry and darted through the open door, screaming in pain. One terrorist's body had been booby-trapped with a grenade. Luckily, our soldiers were safe, because they had followed the SOP of tying a rope around the corpse and pulling out the body only after getting behind cover.

Yet, although we were over a hundred metres away, a couple of splinters had hit Subedar Bodh Raj's back. He was not seriously wounded. But it struck me that I too could have been hit by the splinters as we were standing side by side, shoulder to shoulder at the doorway, looking inside. But God has been kind and that was another close shave for me, as it was for Subedar Bodh Raj who escaped with a minor injury.

Is it karma? I don't know, but I have always believed that the good one does comes back to one in this lifetime.

In a soldier's world, the line between life and death is always a thin one. In fact, a soldier usually doesn't even notice when he has narrowly escaped death by a bullet or grenade splinter that has whizzed very close past him. With a prayer of thanks, he continues to fight, without even allowing himself the luxury of feeling relief.

6
A Woman in the Village

My battalion was based on the LoC in Poonch, J&K. As the CO, I travelled to and stayed at all our posts on the LoC. Mostly though I stayed at the battalion base which was located next to a small village near Mandi, the last township before you climbed the Pir Panjal range and crossed northwards into the Kashmir Valley. The village stood next to our camp. The locals in J&K tend to build houses close to army deployments as a reassurance against terrorists.

In the village there lived a woman with three grown-up daughters. Her husband had abandoned her and fled to become a sadhu, or so I was told. Left with no source of income, she and her daughters took to sex work, their clients the many soldiers who lived away from their families.

I had heard that this brothel had been a cause of disciplinary issues in the battalion we had relieved. Their CO told me that he used to help the women with some rations and money, yet the women were often exploited. Sometimes an errant soldier would get drunk and there would be rowdy fights as well.

When my unit moved in, I ensured strict discipline in this matter. But I wasn't wholly successful. After a few months there were a couple of cases of soldiers frequenting the woman's house. There were also some fights. I would punish those soldiers, sometimes less, sometimes more, to make an example of them. But it had no effect. This affected the discipline, and thus the morale of my battalion.

I decided to tackle the issue head-on. I got the Subedar Major to call the woman to my office one day. I asked her how she could exploit her three daughters for the sake of money and told her that she was setting a poor example in their small village, where everyone knew everyone.

Her replies were direct, candid and forceful. She said, 'Sir, which mother would like to exploit her daughters like this, unless she's pushed to it. I have no source of income; we are five mouths to feed (she had a fourth daughter who was eight or nine years old), and my eldest daughter has been thrown out of her home by her in-laws.

'And, CO sahab, you talk of a bad example for the village; this village didn't help me when I needed their help, when my husband left me. They exploited me, and later my daughters too, in the garb of helping me. Even their wives know what these men are doing.'

She spoke with conviction. I could tell she was not lying. I said, 'If I give you enough for your needs, will you stop your business?' She said, 'You will provide for us today, CO sahab, but what will happen after you go? I'll be back where I was.' I sensed I was losing the argument. Subedar Major Romesh Chander and Regimental Police (RP) Havildar Surjit Singh, who had brought her to my office, were listening to me. I had kept them there as witnesses to avoid any chances of her making accusations later.

I also knew that there was a crowd of office runners, clerks, cooks, soldiers and others, within earshot and out of it, bursting with curiosity to know what had transpired between their CO and Simran (name changed).

I tried to raise the ante, but it did not work. She said that in the middle of the night when someone started banging on her door, no one came to help. Neighbours only hurled abuses. Such behaviour would not stop. Women staying alone in a small village would always be exploited.

I spontaneously asked her, 'What if I get your elder daughter settled back in her in-laws' house?'

She replied, *'CO sahab, roz thwade pair dho ke piyangi.'* We had been conversing in Punjabi all along, and translated what she said means 'I'll wash your feet and drink that water every day'. It's the ultimate expression of gratitude.

Simran had had to bear a double stigma in the conservative rural society she lived in. She was not just a single mother who didn't have a man in the house to protect her, but her married daughter had also been thrown out of her husband's home because she could not fulfil the agreed terms of dowry.

I had spoken without thinking and had no idea how I was going to accomplish this. But I could see that she had softened, and I decided to grab the opportunity. 'Do you want your eight-year-old to be exploited when she should be playing and studying? You'll make her a woman before her time.' That touched her. Her youngest was studying in school.

I then told her to give me some time to find a solution, but that in the meantime her door should stay locked. We would provide her with rations and some money. Our unit would also make it known to every soldier and every villager that her house was out of bounds for them. As a CO, I could ensure that much for a few days, especially for a good cause.

I was from the JAK LI regiment, hence all the soldiers in my paltan were from J&K. I used that to my advantage and found relatives of her daughter's husband in my battalion. We tried everything in the book and outside it to sort out matters between her and her in-laws.

Luckily, we succeeded. Most of the credit for this breakthrough goes to Subedar Major Romesh Chander. He was a mature JCO and a superb mediator who worked hard to convince the husband's family to forgo the dowry. In rural communities, this was tough to pull off, but it helped that our battalion had soldiers, both serving as well as retired, from that village.

When her daughter went back to live with her

husband in her in-laws' house, Simran's joy knew no bounds. She came to thank me with tears in her eyes. Then I made her another offer. I asked her if she would like to be a Special Police Officer to be posted at our unit main gate, which was also a thoroughfare for Mandi town. We needed a female officer to check the women passing through the gate.

I had spoken to the Superintendent of Police and arranged for an additional vacancy, as the woman constable assigned to our unit was irregular in reporting for duty. Simran did not know what to say. She was dumbstruck when I told her that from being exploited, she would now go on to help enforce the law.

She was a well-built, strong woman, and in the police khaki salwar suit, she looked every bit the cop. Her dealings with difficult customers and hostile neighbours had given her enough experience to handle all kinds of people, language and rude behaviour. Her loyalty too was beyond suspicion for obvious reasons. In short, she was an effective policewoman at the gate.

My three years of command roughly coincided with my battalion's posting in that location. By the time my tenure ended, Simran's second daughter had also been married off, with some help from the paltan. The paltan subsequently moved to Damana, near Jammu. It was providential; I could use the contacts of our unit soldiers to settle Simran near our paltan location. It gives me tremendous satisfaction to know that the army made a difference to the lives of a woman and her four daughters.

Simran had to bear a double stigma in the conservative rural society she lived in. She was not just a single mother who didn't have a man in the house to protect her, but her married daughter had also been thrown out of her husband's home because she could not fulfil the agreed terms of dowry.

7

If You Get There Alive, You Will Live

If you get there alive, you will live.

Isn't that a fantastic motto for a hospital? This is no marketing jingle; it's what anyone who has walked through this hospital's doors will tell you. For me, it counts as India's most special medical institute. Where is it? What is it called? I can hear you ask. Read on ...

Most cases in a hospital come from lifestyle diseases. This hospital gets more trauma cases than lifestyle diseases. Trauma cases are typically from road accidents or burn-related injuries. In this hospital, patients come in with gunshot wounds, injuries from landmine blasts and grenade, rocket and artillery splinter injuries. Diabetes or heart attack cases are rare here; what's common are hypothermia, high-altitude pulmonary oedema, frostbite, chilblains. Walk through the corridors and you'll probably hear a doctor say, 'Congratulations, you only lost your foot.'

Welcome to the Army Base Hospital at Badami Bagh Cantonment in Srinagar, Kashmir. Since Independence, we have had soldiers deployed on the LoC with Pakistan, where casualties of the type described above are an occupational hazard. Sadly, over the last three or more decades, the violence has escalated on both the LoC and in the Kashmir Valley because of the rise of terrorism. And the Base Hospital has become busier and more important than ever.

The hospital has risen to the challenge. Every soldier deployed in Kashmir knows that if he can get to this hospital alive, he will be saved. That's how good its medical care is and how dedicated its doctors and staff are. It's difficult to live up to such a reputation, but those who are posted to this hospital get influenced by its ethos and find themselves determined to keep up the good work.

The drills and SOPs of this hospital have evolved and been perfected with time. I must describe how the battle procedure of these medical warriors starts.

As soon as the helicopter carrying a casualty lifts off from the action area, a siren is sounded in the hospital. Immediately the staff – doctors, surgeons, anaesthetists, nurses, nursing assistants, the ward staff, support staff – start converging at their stations.

The Base Hospital is not located in one building. As it happens in the hills, it is made up of a cluster of buildings, big and small. It helps that the walking paths on the slopes between buildings get you from one place to the other far more quickly than going by car on the longer road between the buildings.

Since it is located in an operational zone, the hospital staff are always overworked and are ready to be on duty at odd hours. Even their residential buildings are located right next to the hospital units. Despite the extra work and the gruelling hours they put in, they are all very kind and patient with the patients.

During the summer of 2016, the Valley was on the boil after we had eliminated all the top terrorist leaders, most notably Burhan Wani. There were large-scale protests and stone pelting every day. We were getting more casualties than we could handle and had to improvise a third makeshift operation theatre. Police and Central Reserve Police Force (CRPF) casualties also wanted to be treated there because of its reputation, so the hospital was bursting at the seams. Doctors and paramedics willingly and cheerfully worked round the clock.

Once a Squadron Leader of the Indian Air Force reported to the hospital. He said he was a surgeon and happened to be on holiday in Gulmarg with his family. When he heard of the extra load on the hospital through a batchmate, he volunteered to come and contribute. He worked for three days, helping out in many surgeries, despite being on a well-earned leave. The better part of his vacation with his family was spent in the operation theatre.

During that period, we modified an Advanced Landing Helicopter (ALH) into a makeshift ambulance. So whenever there was an encounter with terrorists or an operation began on the LoC or in the hinterland, the chopper was loaded with basic medical equipment, medicines and other necessary materials and had a paramedic. Now the casualties could be given medical aid from the word go, as soon they arrived at the evacuation helipad. Getting medical help at the right time can save a wounded soldier's life, and we saved a lot of soldiers this way.

Contrast this with the practice in my younger days, when we could evacuate a casualty by helicopter only during the day. So the wounded soldier had to wait at the LoC or in the area of operation till the next morning, as most operations took place during the night. Sometimes the weather would play truant the next day which would delay things further.

Quite often we would start evacuating the casualty by land, which involved carrying him down in a stretcher, walking for hours on the mountains through snow or heavy forest or both and then finally getting the victim to an ambulance after reaching a road.

In 2016, ALH Mark-II, which had night-flying capability, were inducted in the Valley. This meant casualties could now be evacuated 24/7. It was a boon for the soldiers, a reassurance that hadn't been there before. However, it also meant that the medical warriors had to work 24/7.

But they were not complaining. They were happy that they could save more wounded soldiers. I learnt that on days when multiple military operations were taking place, they would anticipate casualties coming in and ensure their doctors and paramedic staff took breaks early in the day so they could be fresh and ready to work long hours when the soldiers were flown in.

Once after a particularly violent military operation, I went to the helipad to meet the casualties. As their stretchers were being transferred from the helicopter to the ambulance, I told a young soldier, '*Himmat rakhna, beta, sab theek ho jayega* (Have courage, son, everything will be all right).' He had multiple gunshot wounds and had lost a lot of blood, but he was conscious, although weak. 'He replied, '*Ab koi darr nahin, sahab, main toh yahaan zinda pahunch gaya hoon; ab toh jeeyunga bhi, aur phir se ladunga bhi* (Now I am not afraid, sir. I have reached here alive. Now I will live to fight again)!'

What a sentiment! What josh!

⌐Most cases in a hospital come from lifestyle diseases. In this hospital, diabetes or heart attack cases are rare; what's common are gunshot wounds, injuries from landmine blasts, grenade splinter injuries, high-altitude pulmonary oedema, frostbite.⌐

8

Don't Call the Soldier

When I was commanding my battalion on the LoC in J&K, my family stayed in Jammu. In the Indian Army, when a soldier is posted to a non-family station, his family can stay at a station of their own choice, in what is known as separated family accommodation. I was allotted a house in Sunjuwan Cantonment on the bypass road near Bhatindi.

A row of twelve houses had been earmarked as separated family accommodation. Mine was a corner house with a huge mango tree in front. All officers whose families were staying in this row were posted in different parts of J&K, which has mostly non-family army stations.

For the benefit of the families, the army

authorities installed a booth under the mango tree in which was installed a real object of desire – a telephone connected to the army lines of communication. The officers could speak to their families and vice versa. Please remember, in those days – I'm talking about the 1990s – there were no mobile phones, and even landlines were fairly uncommon. Besides, it was hard to connect to army units in operational areas of J&K through the commercial landlines.

This phone and the phone booth were therefore a lifeline. Once when I was on leave I noticed that in the evenings the area became like the village square. Ladies would come to the phone booth to make and receive calls, chatting with each other while waiting for their turn, children would cycle or play as they waited to talk to their fathers. It had become the social centre of the cantonment.

But the atmosphere wasn't always so cheerful. Sometimes there was bad news. If someone had been injured in a firefight with terrorists or the enemy on the LoC, it darkened everyone's mood. Even the children would go silent. They could somehow guess the mood without being told the news.

Bad news did not come often. But what did frequently linger around the mango tree was an atmosphere of suspense. Whenever an encounter started somewhere in the state, whether it was in Poonch or Rajauri or Doda, word would travel to the cantonment. Families knew something was happening, but since there were no mobile phones, details were not easy to come by until someone telephoned.

During an encounter or operation, the unit does not entertain any call from outside; even the CO is not allowed to attend a call from his wife. So the women would anxiously wait for some news, some clarity about which area the operation was taking place in and whether their husbands' unit was involved. The suspense remained until they learnt that all was well. The anxiety and tension would be defused, only to rise again the next day or the next week.

My family stayed in that cantonment for over three years. Three years and three months of suspense around the mango tree with a phone booth. Two decades on, I visited the area as a retired officer with my wife and we went to that house. There was no phone booth any more.

The unit there had informed the officer occupying our old house of our visit, and he graciously invited us inside. We met the two families who lived there and laughingly told them about the phone booth, trying to describe what it had meant to us. I could see that they could not fully grasp the importance of the phone booth in our lives in those pre-mobile-phone days!

Communication, and a delay in it, no longer creates suspense. In fact, now there is an excess of communication, and that creates its own problems.

Don't Call the Soldier

Soldiers have mobile phones, their families have mobile phones, everyone does. In these days of instant accessibility, there is no concept of 'sleeping over things'. The moment something agitates or excites someone, there is an urge for spontaneous sharing. This is not always healthy.

There have been instances when a soldier's wife has had a difference of opinion with her in-laws, something that is commonplace. Instead of 'cooling off', she immediately picks up her mobile phone and calls her husband, who may be on an important assignment.

If a soldier is on duty, let us say in an operational area, and gets such calls often while dealing with his responsibilities and operational pressures, it can create additional problems. After all, these soldiers always carry firearms in operational areas; they need to be calm and focused, not agitated or worried about domestic discord.

I have always insisted that soldiers not carry

mobiles in their pockets during duty hours. Soldiers who harm themselves or others are often those who get some disturbing news from the home front, something which in the past would have perhaps sorted itself out by the time someone thought of picking up a pen to write a letter about it. There have also been instances when someone's phone has rung while he has been patrolling on the LoC, thus giving away his position, as our troops are often positioned extremely close to the Pakistani troops on the LoC at several places.

Once a soldier in my battalion was behaving very oddly on returning from leave. My Subedar Major reported that he was aggressive and moody, even quarrelsome. He was threatening his peers and even his seniors at times. Once after he got into a bitter argument with his Platoon Havildar over allocation of duties, the Havildar closed the discussion by threatening to report him to the Company Commander for insubordination.

Seething with fury, he said to his friends over lunch that some day he would kill the Havildar and dump his body in the nala on the LoC so that his body would float off to Pakistan. On other occasions, he would be withdrawn and irritable. These were dangerous signs and his Platoon Commander felt he could harm others or himself. We had heard of such attempts in other units.

The company wanted to send him to the battalion base where he could be given sedentary duties without a weapon. As is the norm, he was brought in for an interview with me before being sent away. There were about eight or ten other soldiers waiting for their CO interview as well. They were there for different reasons – someone going for a training course or on leave, someone who had excelled in an operation. I used to step outside my office, stand in front of the interview parade, as it is called, and talk to the soldiers one by one.

I had instructed the Subedar Major to have this

soldier placed at the end of the line, so that he would be the last man I talked to that day. When I finished interviewing everyone, I came to Rifleman Trilok Singh (name changed) and said, '*Haan, Trilok, kya problem hai* (What's the problem)?'

He replied, '*Kuchh nahin, sahab* (Nothing, sir).'

'I heard you've been threatening people in your company post, saying you'll shoot anyone who acts funny with you?' He uttered a meek no, but was clearly agitated and fidgety. '*Yeh sab mere ko tang karte hain* (They all trouble me).'

I said sharply and loudly, 'Does that mean you will shoot someone? Whom do you want to shoot? SM sahab here, or me? Who else?' I took the rifle from an armed soldier who was standing nearby and thrust it into his hands. 'Go ahead, shoot! Shoot whoever you want. *Chalao goli*,' I said.

There was pin-drop silence. Everyone was stunned. A soldier from the QRT who was standing in front of the Adjutant Office moved in front of me to try and protect me. I waved him off. Other soldiers on parade were apprehensive; a few clerks talking softly in the corridor froze like statues.

All eyes, including mine, were locked on Trilok. Trilok didn't know how to react. He fidgeted for a bit, then it looked as if he was going to cock the weapon, for which contingency I had briefed the RP Havildar, who was prepared to snatch the weapon from him.

Then Trilok crumbled. He said, '*Galti ho gayi, sir* (I've made a mistake, sir).' I took the rifle away, put my arm around his shoulder and said, 'I'm like your elder brother, tell me what's bothering you. Let's go into my office.' He had tears in his eyes.

Later, in the presence of the Subedar Major, he opened up about a domestic quarrel, some financial issues, and his (perceived) victimization by the Company Havildar Major, who he felt was giving him all the tough tasks. We talked to him and reassured him. The Subedar Major even offered to mediate in his domestic issues, if need be. Rifleman Trilok Singh left my office with far more peace of mind than he had had in days.

Later that night, in the Officers' Mess, the Unit Medical Officer asked me, 'Sir, since he was somewhat unstable, what if he had opened fire at everyone there?' I smiled, 'In that case, I would certainly have been court-martialled for giving him a weapon.'

Then why did I risk it, he wanted to know. To which I replied, 'The bullets had been taken out of the rifle that was given to him. I obviously can't risk the lives of everyone.'

Every situation in the field throws up its own dynamics, and there are no set-piece solutions. I often wonder what would have happened if Trilok had tried to fire the rifle at me or others. While no harm would have been caused, as there were no bullets in the magazine, would he have been guilty of manslaughter? I haven't been able to answer that yet.

I have always insisted that soldiers not carry mobiles in their pockets during duty hours. Soldiers who harm themselves or others are often those who get some disturbing news from the home front, something which in the pre-mobile-phone past would have sorted itself out by the time someone thought of picking up a pen to write a letter about it.

9

Catching a Snake

The Indian Army's commando course is one of the toughest in the world. The training lasts for over thirty-three days and is designed to make the soldier incredibly strong, both mentally and physically. The course culminates in a jungle trip where the soldier has to live off the land in extremely harsh terrain. This exercise, designed to physically and mentally break the soldier, is regarded as the hardest part of the course. Such was the rigour of the training that after going through it, most of the soldiers felt they could survive and win in the toughest of situations.

In the early 1980s, I was posted as a Commando Instructor in the Infantry School at Belgaum. Being a bit of a maverick, I used to train the attendees to catch snakes and cut, cook and eat them as part of the jungle survival practice.

The technique was tricky. You had to use a forked stick to catch the snake by its neck and then hold its neck to prevent it from biting. Cobras are the favoured snake for this demonstration. The snakes are neither defanged nor drugged, though there are occasions when the demonstration is done using non-venomous snakes because poisonous snakes can't be found.

This demonstration was also conducted for NCC cadets and students of military schools. During one such demonstration for around 300 students at an all-India military school camp, I was asked to show them how to catch a snake with an ordinary stick if a forked stick could not be found.

While conducting this training, one of the boys asked, 'Sir, that's a non-poisonous snake. Can you catch a poisonous snake with a straight stick?' I used

Catching a Snake

to catch poisonous snakes like cobras and vipers only with a forked stick. Normally one would not try a straight stick on a cobra. Since it was risky, we gave this demo on a rat snake because it was non-poisonous. This was the SOP.

But I thought to myself that these young students would go back to their schools in different parts of the country and talk deprecatingly about a Commando Instructor being scared to catch a cobra in the manner that he preached. So, much against my good sense, I went ahead and tried to catch one. I managed to do it, but it wasn't easy. They all clapped. And I, who had held my breath, heaved a sigh of relief. The next day I was hauled up by my Commandant for acting rashly. 'Do you think you're a bloody hero?'

Fast-forward fifteen years. I had moved up and was commanding my battalion on the LoC in J&K. In one of the many terrorist encounters my unit faced, I lost an officer, Major Rohit Sharma, whom I wrote about in chapter 2. He was awarded a Shaurya Chakra posthumously, and as is the norm in the army, I had to escort his widow for the investiture ceremony at Rashtrapati Bhavan, where the President of India bestows the awards.

At the rehearsal one day prior to the investiture ceremony, we were briefed about the award ceremony by the Aide-de-Camp (ADC) to the President of India. He was a tall and smart army officer, who introduced himself as Captain Gopi Singh Rathore.

When the practice was over, he walked up to me and said, 'Sir, you won't recognize me, but I was the student who asked you to catch a cobra with a straight stick fifteen years ago. Many years later, when I did the commando course as a Lieutenant, I realized how childish I was to ask such a thing of you, and how brave you were.'

We kept in touch after that. When I was posted to Delhi a couple of years later, he once invited my family and me to Rashtrapati Bhavan and gave us a grand tour as his personal guests. He even showed us around a couple of places where visitors were not usually permitted. I was particularly impressed by his passion and knowledge about plants and flowers as he walked us through the famous Mughal Garden.

I read somewhere that President K.R. Narayanan admired the way the young soldier would talk about the gardens to the foreign dignitaries who visited Rashtrapati Bhavan. I believe he often told Gopi that he should have become a horticulturist. Gopi served K.R. Narayanan for four years and continued in his post as ADC to the next president, Dr A.P.J. Abdul Kalam.

During our visit to Rashtrapati Bhavan, Gopi gifted me his recently published book of poems called *Aaj se Pehle* (Before Today). It came as a pleasant surprise to me that this soldier was also a poet, a rare combination in the army. I learnt from his officers much later that Prime Minister Atal Bihari Vajpayee had personally corrected his collection of poems. Gopi also published a collection of short stories called *Aur Kya Chahiye?* (What Else Does One Want?).

He came to our home a couple of times and endeared himself to the whole family. My schoolgoing sons really looked up to this tall and smart captain. He was really a hero-like figure. Not only was he charming, bright and well read, but he had also stood first in the order of merit in the Indian Military Academy and was awarded the coveted gold medal in his course.

After nearly five years in Rashtrapati Bhavan as ADC to two presidents, he longed to get back into the thick of action. He told President Kalam that he wanted to serve in the Kashmir Valley and got posted to 14 Rashtriya Rifles Battalion in Bandipora, J&K. He acquitted himself with such bravery that he was fondly called Eagle by his battalion.

K.R. Narayanan died on 9 November 2005. Gopi was in tears on hearing about his death – the former president had been a father figure to him. Despite his grief, he could not go to Delhi for the cremation, as his unit was in the middle of counter-insurgency operations in Kashmir. The young soldier was disappointed, but he understood that duty came first.

The next day, on 10 November, he led an operation to flush out terrorists holed up in a building at Bandipora. During the operation, Gopi displayed utmost bravery and killed a terrorist in a close combat situation, but paid with his life.

Mr Gopal Gandhi, then governor of West Bengal, who had been secretary to the President when Gopi was ADC, remarked, 'The President takes his ADC along.' Gopi was awarded the Shaurya Chakra posthumously.

His death was one of the rare occasions in the Valley when a bandh was declared in Bandipora as a mark of respect. Gopi had had a good rapport with the locals. He was very approachable and was always ready to lend a helping hand to those willing to pursue the right path, just as he was ruthless in tackling terrorists.

The famous actress Anushka Sharma, whose father, Colonel Ajay Kumar Sharma (Retired), is from the same battalion as Gopi, wrote a touching obituary for him called 'My Hero for Life'.

This is an excerpt from a letter that she wrote on 6 December 2007.

> Tall, dark, handsome, intelligent, funny, loving, honest, compassionate, successful, brave. Isn't this the picture every young girl has in mind for her Prince Charming, knight in shining armour, etc., along with her belief in fairy tales and Santa Claus? But by the time we girls reach adolescence we realize that this perfect person does not really exist, not in the real world. We come to terms with

reality and tell ourselves that nothing is perfect. Santa Claus, Tooth Fairy, Cinderella, Prince Charming, Snow White are soon forgotten. Like every other girl I too believed in these things, like my friends I also grew up and laughed at my foolishness. But things turned out differently for me. I happened to be one of the lucky ones to see that perfect man of every little girl's dream. He was everything we imagine a man to be. He was my Gopi uncle, better known as Major Gopi Singh Rathod. An army officer with so many distinguished qualities and achievements. I find myself too short in stature to talk about [him].

Ten years after Gopi's supreme sacrifice, I became the Corps Commander in Srinagar. I was delighted to see that a Major Gopi Singh Rathore, Shaurya Chakra (Posthumous), Memorial Football Tournament was still being held in Bandipora every year in his honour.

One of his unit officers recalled that Gopi probably had a premonition of his short life. He had once teasingly asked this brave young officer why he didn't get married. Gopi's reply was, 'Sir, I wish I had a long life.' A few months later he laid down his life for the nation.

In the army we hold on to our memories of colleagues, the conversations we had with them and the battles fought alongside them more strongly and closely than we do the memories of our families.

A salute to the braveheart!

As a Commando Instructor, I used to train the attendees to catch snakes and cook and eat them as part of the jungle survival practice.

10

Tough Times Don't Last, Tough People Do

'We make men out of boys' reads a large board at the entrance of the Commando Wing, the Infantry School, Belgaum, a town on the western coast of India that lies between Panaji and Kolhapur. It is here that India's fittest and finest soldiers undergo a thirty-three-day commando course designed to test their endurance to the limit, both emotionally and physically. If they pass it, they enter the elite of the Indian armed forces.

The Indian Army commando course is considered one of the toughest in the world. When I was posted here as a Commando Instructor in the mid-1980s, an American officer left the course midway saying it was inhuman. Most Indian officers who go for their

'Rangers' course – the American equivalent of the Indian commando course – end up doing very well, and several of our officers have topped the course.

During the commando course, special skills are imparted to the soldiers. It's all about the extremes your body and mind can handle. The commandos (as the students are known, be they officers or soldiers) are constantly reminded that *tough times don't last, but tough people do*.

Weapon training is the bread and butter of a soldier. While firing skills mark the foundation for any soldier, it is his expertise in this that graduates him into becoming a commando. In advanced stages of weapon training, a soldier learns how to strip or assemble a rifle or pistol blindfolded.

Why does he need to do this? Because there may be a defect in his gun at night, or he may not be able to use his torchlight for fear of being spotted by the enemy. He must thus have the ability to be able to rectify the fault in the dark. He is also trained in ambidextrous firing (using both hands and shoulders), firing on the move and peripheral-vision firing. These disciplines of firing are essential for the survival of a commando and help him in various combat situations.

Basic military training for any soldier also includes physical fitness. In the commando course, these skills are honed to the next level. In the course, commandos are trained to jump from twelve-foot-high walls, walk on narrow platforms and beams fifty feet high, slither down from helicopters hovering fifteen metres above the ground and run long distances of ten, twenty, thirty and forty kilometres progressively, while carrying their complete battle load and personal weapons of twenty-two and a half kilos. By the end of the course, they're basically running a marathon carrying a heavy load.

Speed marches, as these endurance runs against time are called, are a gruelling exercise. An even more gruelling training session is marching across country as part of a team carrying out a mock raid or attack. Once while walking with a team (one instructor always accompanies the commandos to bring out the lessons learnt from the training session), I recall seeing two commandos lying down flat next to a stream and lapping up the water like animals – that was the level of thirst and fatigue.

The aim of this extreme endurance training is to test whether the human mind can triumph over the human body. I recall a few instances where soldiers did not let fractures deter them from completing their route march so that their teams would not be disqualified. This is only training, you might feel, why do they have to kill themselves to win? It's not war, so why is it so important to win? It is a question of attitude. In my profession there are no runners-up. Those who don't win often end up dead.

At the end of the course, small teams are formed and sent into jungles and mountains to strengthen their jungle survival techniques. This final challenge is the hardest of all. During such exercises, the commandos' biological clocks are reversed – they operate in the night (most operations behind enemy lines are conducted under cover of darkness) and rest by day, that too in turns. They are made to do things they haven't done before.

Commandos are taught how to draw water out of a succulent cactus or the sap of a tree by placing a polythene sheet overnight in a manner that it collects water through condensation by morning. They learn to cook directly over fire in the absence of a cooking range and pots and pans by wrapping foodstuff in a broad banana leaf or other such leaves and then covering it in a mud paste. This is how one can roast or bake meat, depending on what you can catch.

As part of the jungle survival practice, among other subjects, I used to train the commandos to catch snakes and cut, cook and eat them, as mentioned in chapter 9. Why snakes, you might ask. Surprisingly, a snake is easy to catch, cut and cook, and it is tasty, just like fish. Once you learn how to do it, you realize how tough it is to catch a deer or a hare or even a junglefowl without help.

At the end of four days, the commandos are put through an interesting exercise to give them practice in escape and evasion. They are told that they are prisoners of war who have escaped from the prison. They have to return to the commando school fifty-odd kilometres away, while all the instructors and staff act as the enemy looking for them.

If they are caught, they are taken a few kilometres further in a vehicle and set free, only to start all over again. The commandos do this in buddy pairs. They also have to fend for food by using all the jungle survival techniques taught to them. Prudence lies in sticking to mountain and jungle routes, as the instructors tend to be near roads. Needless to say, that's much harder!

Several commandos come up with ingenious

methods to deal with this challenge. When I was training to be a commando, two of my batchmates did not return from the exercise at all. A whole day passed with no news of them. We were all beginning to get a little worried.

Later in the night, they returned sheepishly and related their tale. They got too creative and caught a bus in their fatigues and battle loads. To escape detection, they climbed up to the rooftop luggage rack. Utterly exhausted, they drifted into a deep sleep, and did not wake up until the bus reached its destination – Goa! Never before had anyone been so regretful of taking a bus to this holiday destination!

I have been a Commando Instructor, and so I get carried away when I talk about the course. But the truth is that we lay a lot of emphasis on training in general in the Indian Army. As a result, it's a very professional force.

Have you ever wondered why it is that whenever there is a disaster, natural or man-made, the army is called to help? While the army is the instrument of last resort, it often ends up being the first responder, despite the fact that there are several forces and organizations like the National Disaster Response Force (NDRF), the State Disaster Response Fund (SDRF) and other paramilitary troops. Essentially, we live, and die, by the old adage, *'The more you sweat in peace, the less you will bleed in war.'*

Talking of blood and sweat, allow me to end with an anecdote about both. As a Commando Instructor, there was one python I used to catch a couple of times a week while giving demonstrations to students or visiting dignitaries.

Normally, a snake would be restless if I caught its tail or tapped its head with a stick. However, the python was surprisingly comfortable when I would hold it with a stick or catch its neck. In fact, after a while it would slither towards its terrarium once I had finished the demonstration, without me needing to put it back.

Once when I was giving the demonstration, I caught the python's tail with my right hand and was about to press its head down with a stick when someone asked me a question. The snake's head was still free. Its familiarity and docility had made me a bit casual. When I turned to answer the question, the snake suddenly turned around and bit my finger.

I quickly caught its neck with my left hand. It coiled the rest of its body around my arm. The situation was complicated. My finger was in its mouth, its mouth was in my other hand and its body was coiled around both my hands, squeezing my right arm.

The blood and sweat were making my grip slippery. The python is a non-poisonous snake but its teeth are shaped like a sewing machine and with every bite it swallows its prey in, little by little. After swallowing its prey, the python usually breaks it down by tightly coiling its body around a tree, so that the prey gets crushed.

The zookeeper Mani came to my rescue. Even he was a little tentative, and I had to assure him that my grip over the snake's neck was firm. Thus reassured, Mani slowly uncoiled the python's tail. It wasn't easy because the python was squeezing its body tightly in defence because it was scared too. Within a few minutes we managed to disentangle the python, and I threw it into the zoo where it slithered off to its corner. I reported at the military hospital for the necessary shots.

My wedding was scheduled for ten days later. On the day of the wedding, I received a telegram from my colleagues in the Commando Wing saying that the python had died.

Hearing this, my wife very nearly refused to marry me.

⌐ The aim of extreme endurance commando training is to test whether the human mind can triumph over the human body. It is a question of attitude. In my profession there are no runners-up. Those who don't win often end up dead. ⌐

11
The Making of a Hero

He died before he even lived! What else can you say for someone who lays down his life for the country at such a young age?

'Sir, I want to be with the boys,' said a young officer, refusing to go home on sick leave when I met him at the Base Hospital in Srinagar. His jaw had been broken by a stone-pelting crowd.

Pelting stones at security forces is a comparatively recent development. Inspired by the Intifada of Palestine, Kashmiri youth took to it to register their protests from 2008 to 2010, for stone pelting was believed to have better acceptance in the Western world as an unarmed protest.

Later, in 2015, Kashmiris started stone pelting

during encounters between security forces and terrorists. The stone pelters distracted security forces, warned the terrorists in advance and sometimes even assisted them in escaping. While pelters are considered unarmed, stone pelting is violent, viciously violent.

I saw its consequences often. As the Corps Commander of the Srinagar-based 15 Corps, fondly called Chinar Corps, I frequently met patients at the Base Hospital in Badami Bagh Cantonment, the Military Headquarters. I saw all types of cases – gunshot wounds, grenade splinter injuries, terrible frostbite and cases of depression. The injuries caused by stone pelting were no less than any of these.

My soldiers often asked me how to deal with stone pelting, especially when women and children were doing the throwing. I always found this question tough to answer. After all, soldiers have deadly weapons to defend themselves, ones that fire lethal bullets. In inflamed situations, even a single bullet can cause an outbreak. We really depend on the ingenuity and patience of the soldiers and their leaders to get out of these situations without letting them flare up. While handling such tricky conditions, many of our soldiers would get seriously injured.

One such officer was young Captain Pawan Kumar, who I met on 4 or 5 February 2016, while he was admitted at the Base Hospital. He was returning with his team after a successful encounter with terrorists in south Kashmir, where they had eliminated four terrorists.

On their way back, they were surrounded by a mob that started pelting stones at them. Exercising utmost restraint, he extricated his team without firing a single shot, as there were children and women in the mob. However, his restraint meant he was left with a few injuries, including a fractured jaw, which was wired up when I met him.

The CO of the Base Hospital told me that the young man had been advised to go home on four weeks of sick leave, but he was refusing to do so. In the army, if a patient does not require constant medical care but only rest, he is sent home on sick leave.

When I asked him why he did not want to go home, he simply said, 'Sir, I want to be with the boys.' I couldn't help smiling as I looked at this young man who wanted to return to his 'boys', each of whom were trained SF soldiers, all older than him and more experienced. I asked him his age. He was all of twenty-three. He was younger than my younger son, and his enthusiasm was so infectious that I impulsively broke protocol and ruffled his hair, saying, 'Happy hunting, son.'

'Let him do what he wants, doc,' I told the Commandant of the Base Hospital before leaving. A fortnight later, I saluted Pawan's mortal remains in a casket.

The Making of a Hero

I was overwhelmed.

It was a huge operation. The biggest hostage situation during my tenure as General Officer Commanding (GOC) of the Srinagar-based Chinar Corps was on 20 February 2016. Four Lashkar-e-Taiba terrorists armed with AK-47 assault rifles, hand grenades and explosives attacked a CRPF convoy on the main road linking Srinagar to Jammu, killing two policemen and a civilian. The terrorists then took refuge in a huge Entrepreneurship Development Institute building and took scores of hostages.

The first priority of the army was to evacuate civilians to safety. However, the militants responded with automatic gunfire and hand grenades. A fierce battle ensued with heavy exchange of fire from both sides.

Our soldiers rescued over sixty hostages safely, all Kashmiri men and women. I ruefully recalled that it was Kashmiri youth who had injured Pawan, but that did not make him biased or deter him and his comrades. The young captain led his men from the front and engaged the terrorists courageously.

The terrorists were very well prepared. They had blasted off several walls and created obstructions in corridors, sometimes using heavy furniture. This blocked our soldiers when they rushed in and precluded the use of robots and rolling ball cameras that could relay the terrorists' position. Nevertheless, our men entered the building, and in the close combat battle, Captain Pawan Kumar was seriously injured. Refusing to be evacuated, he continued to fight till he could. He later succumbed to his injuries.

Captain Pawan Kumar, Captain Tushar Mahajan and Lance Naik Om Prakash, all commandos, laid down their lives. While I have narrated only Pawan's story as I had met him at the hospital, the others were no less brave. In fact, in every operation, there are always many unsung heroes who acquit themselves with utmost bravery.

The Making of a Hero

Not everyone can be given medals. Captain Pawan Kumar, however, was awarded the Shaurya Chakra gallantry award on 15 August 2016 for his exceptional courage, fighting spirit and supreme sacrifice.

But there is an equally big hero in this story – Captain Pawan's father, Mr Rajbir Singh. He said at his cremation, and ANI reported it in the news, 'I had only one child. I gave him to the army. No father can be prouder.'

Can you expect anything less from the son of such a brave father?

What makes heroes out of simple boys from our country's small towns and villages? A child picks up his first values at home. A boy from Haryana, Pawan was the son of a schoolteacher.

As a child, Pawan was not much into sports and outdoor activities. Initially he wanted to be an engineer. Later, after he finished his schooling, he secured admission in Ramjas College for a BSc in

Maths (Honours). Meanwhile, one of his cousins who had joined the NDA had come home during his vacation. Listening to his cousin's stories of the NDA and army life, Pawan was inspired to join too.

His father told me that he and his wife were initially reluctant to send him into the army. But on his continued insistence, they relented, allowing him to join as an air force cadet only, as they felt army life was more risky. After his interview at the Services Selection Board in Mysore, he went to Bangalore for the medical tests. There he was rejected temporarily because his eyesight did not meet the required standards, and he had to appear for another medical examination. He then rang up his father and pleaded with him to let him apply for the army as he met the medical standards of the army.

In the face of Pawan's persistence and enthusiasm, his father gave in. I think Pawan was hell-bent on joining the army. When he decided to take the entrance exam for the NDA, he was grossly overweight. It is a tribute to his determination that he reduced his weight by twenty-two kilos, from eighty-six kilos to sixty-four kilos – no mean feat. That was when his father realized his son had true grit.

Pawan was commissioned in December 2013 into 7 Dogra, an excellent battalion. While he was happy to be in the infantry, Pawan aspired to become a Para Commando. But his CO was reluctant to let him go because he did not want to lose a good officer.

Pawan was the cross-country team captain, and during the championship he took his team to victory. Pleased with the team's performance, and with Pawan's role in it, the CO consented to young Pawan applying for a change into an SF unit.

On 28 February 2015, Pawan reported to a Para (SF) Battalion in the desert for a three-month probation training and test. The probation is extremely gruelling, testing your physical endurance, mental robustness and tactical abilities, not to mention weapon handling and firing, under stress and strain.

The young soldier came out with flying colours and he was accepted as an SF officer of the elite Para (SF) Battalion who were trained specially for desert warfare. Donning his maroon beret and the commando's Balidan badge, Captain Pawan Kumar's deepest wish had come true.

He would write animatedly about his training and experiences to his father. His father recalls how thrilled he was when he learnt to parachute in the training school at Agra, and what a high he felt jumping from an aircraft mid-air. The young soldier had a real thirst for challenges. In September, Pawan was deployed with his team in the counter-terrorist operations in J&K.

His father remembers that it was on 3 or 4 October 2015 that Pawan participated in his first encounter with terrorists, and they had a very successful operation. The young Para Commando had moved from the harsh but clean world of training into the real world of blood, sweat and tears. He was now baptized into combat. In January 2016 he came home on leave to celebrate his birthday. As a true soldier, he decided to celebrate it by attending the Raising Day of 7 Dogra, the battalion he was commissioned in.

It is a happy coincidence that Pawan's birthday, the Raising Day of 7 Dogra and Army Day, all fall on 15 January. He travelled with his family and friends, nine of them, to Firozepur to attend the celebrations. It shows how committed he was to his battalion. The fact that he took everyone along for the event also shows his closeness to his family and friends.

As I interacted with his father, I slowly began to understand how Pawan was motivated to join the army, how he set about it with determination and how he became fearless. But I wondered how his father was brave enough to say during his son's last rites, 'I had only one child. I gave him to the army. No father can be prouder.'

When I mentioned this to him he told me that when his son was commissioned, he was touched by the inscription on the Gaurav Padak medal that he and all the other parents were given during the commissioning ceremony that follows the Passing Out Parade. A simple but powerful sentence is inscribed on the medal: *Meri santan desh ko samarpit* (I dedicate my child to the country)! Can you expect anything less from the son of such a brave father.

In just two years of his service in the army, young Pawan was commissioned into the Dogra Regiment and moved up to the highly competitive SF. He died a year later. In that brief time, he won the hearts of his Dogra soldiers and his Para Commando colleagues, and left an impact on everyone who came in contact with him, including me.

The Making of a Hero

I think heroes are shaped by their upbringing at home and school. The army training polishes them and their officers inspire them by leading from the front, but the values that make a hero are instilled at home. How often have we heard words of incredible courage and fortitude from the family, even the children, of these heroes! Matching their words with deeds, several widows of such bravehearts have joined the very army their husbands gave their lives to so they can continue the saga of bravery.

Our young leaders do us proud. Always. But their parents and family do no less.

⌐ What makes heroes out of simple boys from our country's small towns and villages? A child picks up his first values at home. Captain Pawan was the son of a schoolteacher. At his cremation, his father said, 'I had only one child. I gave him to the army. No father can be prouder.' ⌐

12

Bad News

You get trained in the army for everything. But there's one thing no soldier is ever taught – how to break the news of the death of a comrade to his family. It's especially hard because most deaths in combat are among soldiers under the age of thirty-five. They leave behind young widows, little children, devastated parents and an unfinished life.

Families understand that death is an occupational hazard for a soldier, more so for an infantry soldier, who fights on the front line, face to face, and hand to hand if need be. But no one is ever prepared for it.

Hardest of all for an officer is the moral responsibility of losing a soldier under his command. The boys are your boys. Every death is a blow you never quite recover from. All army men in commanding positions feel this way. When suicide terrorists struck at Uri and we lost eighteen soldiers, I felt completely responsible. By then I was the Corps Commander in Kashmir; the soldiers who died weren't directly under my command. But it happened on my watch.

Traditionally in the Indian Army, the CO informs the family if the casualty is an officer, while the Subedar Major informs the family of a soldier. Breaking bad news to a family is one of the most painful tasks I have performed. My colleagues and I are prepared for danger, risk, testing our bodies to the extreme. But this is something that one is not – and can never be – trained for.

On 17 June 2000, in an encounter with terrorists near the LoC, we lost Major Pradeep Tathawade, KC (Posthumous), my second in command. He died fighting terrorists bravely in a fierce hand-to-hand combat. After the operation and the debriefing were over, I walked down the thickly wooded mountain track for an hour to the nearest roadhead. From there my Gypsy took me to Poonch in about two hours. There were no mobile phones in those days. My Battalion Headquarters did not even have an STD phone line.

I did not stop at my Battalion Headquarters which was en route. The only thing on my mind was how I would break the news to Pradeep's widow. I kept composing the words in my mind, again and again, trying to make them perfect. But is there a perfect way to break such news?

I went to a PCO booth and placed a call to Mrs Leenata Tathawade. 'Hello Colonel Dua,' she said cheerfully. That made my job even more difficult. How could I tell her that her husband's body would arrive at her home the next day? That she had to put the phone down and prepare for the cremation? How? In a battalion, we all grow up together, officers and men. We are like one big family. Everyone knows each other's wives, shares news from home, news about how the kids are growing up and so on.

When I finally managed to find my voice, I told her hesitantly that there had been an encounter.

'Is he all right?' she interrupted.

'In which Pradeep fought bravely and—'

'He's no more, na?' she screamed.

My shoulders sagged. All at once I felt as if a load had been lifted off my chest. When I said a quiet yes to her, she wailed loudly.

'*Aayeee, aapne unko kyun bheja* (Oh God, why did you have to send him for the operation)?' The load returned, bearing down even harder on me. I was finding it hard to breathe, and it had nothing to do with the suffocatingly small size of the PCO booth. Her cry of pain will remain with me forever. She was not in a condition to talk any more. Frankly, nor was I, as I was dealing with my own grief of having lost a friend and a colleague of nearly two decades.

Bad News

Different people react differently to bad news. Not everyone can be as stoic as Captain Pawan's father, who said at his son's cremation, 'I had only one child. I gave him to the army.' (chapter 11). In fact, sometimes different members of the same family react differently too.

When I went to Jalandhar to the house of Late Major Rohit Sharma, I had a very different experience, but no less poignant. I have written in chapter 2 about the time we lost Rohit in our first encounter with terrorists when I had just been made CO.

When I reached the Sharmas' home in Model Town, a posh locality of Jalandhar, all the family members had very different reactions. Rohit's wife, Nevedita, was a young lady in her mid-twenties. They had been married for only two years. She mostly sat still like a ghost throughout our interaction, even her tears seemed to have dried up.

Rohit's father, a practising doctor, was a broken

man and had little to say, most of which was philosophical. Rohit was the only son. Two of his sisters were married and had families of their own in Chandigarh and Faridabad. The elder sister and her husband were present and trying to understand the necessary army procedures and documentary requirements that I was trying to explain to them.

His mother held my shoulders firmly and shook me as if she blamed me for her son's death. Then she broke down. I simply submitted in front of a mother's grief. Someone seemed to have said something to her, because she told me almost accusingly that her son may have lived if he had been evacuated in time from the encounter site.

Such reactions from the family of fallen soldiers are commonplace. I tried to reassure her that everything possible was done as early as it could have been done. Rohit was a much loved and respected leader of his men.

She was not convinced; which mother would be?

At one point I even said to her, 'Aunty, it was a very tight and close encounter. I was present; it could as well have been me who was hit.' She simply said, '*Par aisa hua toh nahin na, Colonel sahab* (But this did not happen, Colonel).' I just folded my hands and bowed my head in front of a friend's mother's anguish; my eyes were also moist.

Her words shook me. For the next two decades, I felt guilty whenever I lost a soldier under my command in operations. Why had I come back alive when so and so could not? Even after retirement, that feeling never leaves me. Combat does strange things to people. Every day that I live, I feel guilty for being alive.

Breaking bad news to a family is one of the most painful tasks I have performed. My colleagues and I are prepared for danger, risk, testing our bodies to the extreme. But this is something that one is not – and can never be – trained for.

Afterword

I was once asked at an event what I considered the biggest achievement of my career. This was just before I retired, and I looked back at the time I had spent in the army, thinking about some of the events you have read about in this book.

My mind went over the high points – from the now famous surgical strike to the operational successes, awards, promotions and placements. But it wasn't the wins that stood out as I replayed my career. It was the love and affection I received from my soldiers, and my brother officers. A love that was almost like devotion.

Afterword

Most COs have received this love and loyalty from their men, and there is nothing in the world as powerful and moving as these bonds that bind soldiers to each other. I was about to talk of this at the event, but then I changed my mind.

I instead told my audience that the greatest satisfaction for me was the remarriage of the widows of two of my bravehearts who had died during operations.

Twenty-odd years ago I was fortunate to be appointed CO of my battalion that was deployed on the LoC. We had very active counter-terrorism operations over the next three years, in which I sadly lost eight officers and men. One of them was Major Rohit Sharma who was awarded a Shaurya Chakra (Posthumous). Rohit had been married for only two years.

My joy knew no bounds when a young officer, Major Manoj Deshpande, approached me with a proposal to marry Nevedita, the young widow. He was a dynamic officer, brave and humane, liked and respected by his soldiers and superiors alike. He was also a great fan and a friend of Rohit. Convincing parents and family was not easy, but things worked out eventually.

Major Manoj Deshpande was awarded the Vir Chakra in another daring operation during our tenure in that location itself. He later went on to command our Bravest of the Brave Battalion in an operational area in the Northeast. The couple is blessed with two lovely children, a girl and a boy, both young adults now.

The second wedding was of the widow of another brave soldier – Lance Naik Anter Singh, who was awarded the Sena Medal posthumously after an encounter with terrorists. He was survived by his young widow and a two-month-old daughter. During the condolence meet at his village, I met Rajinder Singh, the younger brother of Anter Singh, a soldier from another regiment. He was unhappy

Afterword

in the army and wanted to quit. I helped him do that and he married his sister-in-law, Jasbir Kaur, a cultural norm in his region. Today the couple have two sons. Anter's daughter is married to a serving soldier from the Punjab Regiment while Jasbir Kaur and Rajinder's elder son is in military training at the JAK LI training centre.

Nothing has given me greater joy than this, as you really feel like the head of the family when you are the CO, more so in counter-terrorism operations. The army is a great school, a place where I have learnt everything I know. And above all, it is a family that has given me more friendships, more memories than anything else. What an honour it has been to serve the army and the nation.

Jai Hind.

Acknowledgements

My father always wanted me to write a book. I would tell him, 'I'm too busy soldiering, Dad,' and he would say, 'Then write after you finish soldiering.' This book is for you, Daddy, you've always been a role model for me. Thank you.

I seek the blessings of Sri Aurobindo and the Divine Mother in my first writing venture, and always.

I want to acknowledge the role of my wife, Aradhana, and sons, Adamya and Ardaman, who not only put up cheerfully with my being away for years at a stretch due to my deployments in

Acknowledgements

operational areas, but also for listening to my anecdotes, reading through them and making suggestions. A special note of thanks to my younger son, Ardaman, who is also my manager.

A few close friends encouraged me to write when I was reluctant to put down first-person accounts, but I wish to single out Colonel Anil Nayer, SM**, a Para Commando Officer with two gallantry medals, for reading every word and making valuable suggestions.

I also warmly thank my publisher and editor, Chiki Sarkar, for her expert guidance through the writing of this book.

Finally, I thank all my mentors and superiors, the brave officers and soldiers that I have been fortunate to command, not only in my Bravest of the Brave Battalion, 8 JAK LI (Siachen), but also beyond, throughout my career.

Jai Hind!

THE APP FOR INDIAN READERS

Fresh, original books tailored for mobile and for India. Starting at ₹10.

juggernaut.in

1

CRAFTED FOR MOBILE READING

Thought you would never read a book on mobile? Let us prove you wrong.

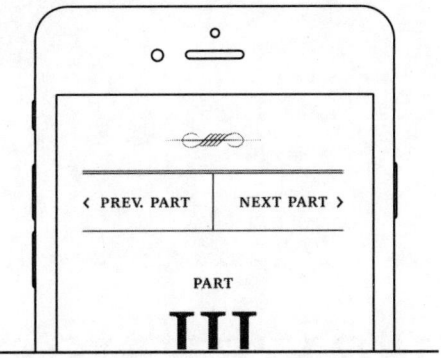

Beautiful Typography

The quality of print transferred
to your mobile. Forget ugly PDFs.

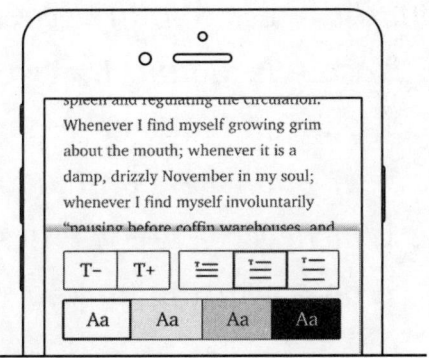

Customizable Reading

Read in the font size, spacing
and background of your liking.

AN EXTENSIVE LIBRARY

Including fresh, new, original Juggernaut books from the likes of Sunny Leone, Praveen Swami, Husain Haqqani, Umera Ahmed, Rujuta Diwekar and lots more. Plus, books from partner publishers and loads of free classics. Whichever genre you like, there's a book waiting for you.

juggernaut.in

3

DON'T JUST READ; INTERACT

We're changing the reading experience from passive to active.

juggernaut.in

Ask authors questions

Get all your answers from the horse's mouth. Juggernaut authors actually reply to every question they can.

Rate and review

Let everyone know of your favourite reads or critique the finer points of a book – you will be heard in a community of like-minded readers.

Gift books to friends

For a book-lover, there's no nicer gift than a book personally picked. You can even do it anonymously if you like.

Enjoy new book formats

Discover serials released in parts over time, picture books including comics, and story-bundles at discounted rates. And coming soon, audiobooks.

juggernaut.in

LOWEST PRICES & ONE-TAP BUYING

Books start at ₹10 with regular discounts and free previews.

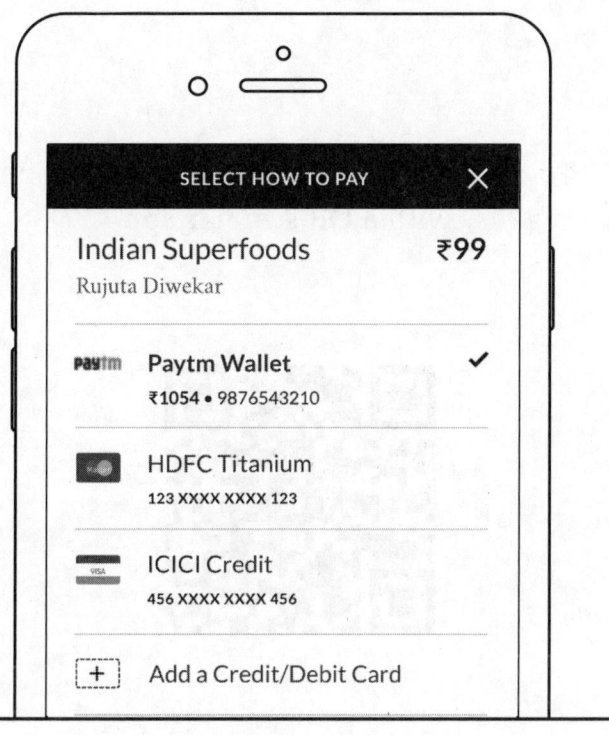

Paytm Wallet, Cards & Apple Payments

On Android, just add a Paytm Wallet once and buy any book with one tap. On iOS, pay with one tap with your iTunes-linked debit/credit card.

To download the app scan the QR Code
with a QR scanner app

For our complete catalogue, visit www.juggernaut.in
To submit your book, send a synopsis and two
sample chapters to books@juggernaut.in
For all other queries, write to contact@juggernaut.in